Activating your

SOULworks

...a healing journey

LAUREN HEISTAD

BALBOA.
PRESS
A DIVISION OF HAY HOUSE

Cover Photo: Dawson Heistad
Author Photo: Kimberley Schmiedge

Balboa Press books may be ordered through booksellers or by contacting:

Balboa Press
A Division of Hay House
1663 Liberty Drive
Bloomington, IN 47403
www.balboapress.com
1 (877) 407-4847

Printed in the United States of America.

ISBN: 978-1-4525-8817-9 (sc)
ISBN: 978-1-4525-8818-6 (hc)
ISBN: 978-1-4525-8816-2 (e)

Library of Congress Control Number: 2013922183

Balboa Press rev. date: 06/20/2017
First Published: 01/21/2014

I dedicate this book to my family and friends (both of this world and the spiritual realm). You have truly given me the courage and support to activate my SOULworks.

ACKNOWLEDGEMENTS

I find myself crying a lot these days. They are not tears of sorrow. They are tears of sheer joy and appreciation for the wonderful people in my life, and the experiences they have brought into my world.

To my mom, Lana: I thank you for being there to help activate my own SOULworks. Thank you for all the support you have provided, and for helping me to discover who I am. It is truly a great mother who can watch her child make their own mistakes, celebrate their own uniqueness, climb their own mountains, and find their own way. You have provided me with more than you will ever know. I am truly grateful to be your daughter.

To my dad, Gary: Thank you for teaching me how to dream big, to always follow those dreams, and to never let anybody tell me what I can or can not accomplish. Whether you realize it or not, you have taught me through your shining example: by never giving up on your own dreams, by always using your intuition, and by courageously breaking new trail by following your heart. I am blessed to watch, learn, and walk beside the footprints of a true dreamer.

To my husband, Scott: Thank you, thank you, thank you. Words cannot truly express my appreciation for all you have done for me. Thank you for continuing to stand by my side as I (not so gracefully), found my way through this journey. Thank you for giving me the time and space I needed to understand myself, embrace myself, and believe in myself. I will forever love you for your kind, patient, and supportive heart.

To my wonderful children, Dawson and Makenna: Thank you for believing in me, even before I could believe in myself. Thank you for always knowing exactly what to say, at exactly the right time. I hope you realize you are wise and loving beyond your years. I look forward to the many adventures to come, and the honor of watching you grow and flourish along your own paths. Thank you for the privilege of being your mom.

To all the unique individuals involved in my spiritual encounters documented within, I am truly grateful. Not only did you inspire and help activate my own SOULworks, but our moments in time were the catalyst I needed to eventually open up and teach what I know. Thank you for the connection we shared, as well as the honor to include those stories within my book.

To those who took a leap of faith and became a part of the SOULworks Sacred Healing Centre, I am so grateful for your dedication and support. Thank you for following your hearts, guidance, and passions. I am grateful to work beside you and am proud to call you my friends.

To all those who have come into my life and provided support, encouragement, and love, I thank you from the bottom of my heart. For those who have trusted me with your health and well-being, I am forever humbled by your trust and open hearts. And for those who have challenged me to be a better person and stand up for what I believe in, thank you and Namaste. There are too many to mention, but you are all in my heart just the same.

To all my dear friends in the spirit world, thank you for your patience and persistence. Thank you for always, always being there for me. Thank you for lending an ear when I needed to talk, for providing a shoulder when I needed to cry, and for offering insights when I needed them most. Thank you for nudging me forward when it was time to speak my truth.

And finally, to the life essence of Yeshua (Jesus): Thank you for being a fundamental and unique part of my own SOULworks. Thank you for reminding me who I am and for providing the encouragement to stand up for that truth. Thank you for breaking ground into uncharted territory and inspiring me to do the same. It is my honor to continue our work, and to assist with the higher calling of ushering in a new world.

FOREWORD

When Lauren asked me to write the forward for this book my first thought was, "This is such an honor." However, if I am to be perfectly honest I need to add that a few years ago, I may not have given the same response. Allow me to explain.

Several years ago, an event in my life was actually the beginning of this incredible journey for Lauren. At the time, I was not even aware of her experience. Of course I knew what happened to me, but it would be many years later before I learned what she experienced that night; and when she did tell me, I am quite sure I did not respond with, "Wow, that is awesome," nor did I rush out to share the story with my friends. At first, I could not even begin to understand it, so I sure wasn't about to try and explain it to anyone else. What would people think? Sure, I believed we all have unique gifts, talents, and abilities. I also believed in angels, but the gifts and abilities Lauren was explaining were way out of my comfort zone.

I wondered why she waited so long to tell me this story and many others. I have since learned it was because of fear and that makes me sad. But I also believe back then, the timing was not right for me to hear it. God (Spirit, the Divine) needed to open my heart and open my mind. As Lauren shared other stories and I witnessed first hand her intuitive healing abilities, I could no longer deny this was very real. I began to ask myself, "Why can't these things happen?" Two thousand years ago, people never questioned an angel visitation, a healing or a vision. It did not make sense to me that these gifts would just disappear. Maybe these gifts and abilities were still within our reach, we had simply lost touch or been taught we could not possibly have such capabilities. What a shame.

I have been privileged to share Lauren's journey and to learn and grow with her. She would be the first to say it has not been easy, but it has been so rewarding. I have learned so much from Lauren and I know beyond a doubt this is just the beginning. She has so many wonderful gifts to share. One of these gifts is to teach others.

You are about to embark on an incredible journey held within the pages of this book. I would ask that you read it with an open heart, an open mind, and a knowing that we can accomplish so much more than we ever thought possible. As you begin your journey to activate your own SOULworks remember to believe. Lauren has shared the following quote with me many times...

"If you believe you can, you are half way there."

Lauren, thank you for giving me the opportunity to write this, I can now say without any hesitation, "This is such an honor." I am so proud of you, and I am so very proud to be your Mom. I love you with all my heart. (Lana Schmiedge)

PREFACE

This book is about my real-life journey as I continue to work my way out of a spiritual closet and activate my SOULworks. The inspirational stories will reveal the ups and downs encountered when finding my true path; the lessons learned, the life changing moments, the challenges, the tribulations, and the personal struggles I encountered when looking for inner peace.

This book is divided into a few different segments as an opportunity to provide not only inspirational stories, but to teach and help others achieve a higher level of understanding and connection to spirit. The format of all chapters follows a three-section layout. Each chapter begins with one of my own unique personal life experiences designed to provide a platform to broaden the awareness and minds of the reader. Each chapter then contains a segment entitled *"Activating Your SOULworks."* This section provides insights and thoughtful explanations regarding the lessons I have learned from each of my experiences. In closing, each chapter ends with a *"Your Move"* portion, encouraging readers to take action on activating their own SOULworks.

Finding my SOULworks has been a very long and challenging process. I invite you to hear my story. *Activating your SOULworks: a healing journey* is about sharing life experiences and challenging others to ponder and activate their own SOULworks.

Please note that within this book I will use the words God, spirit, spirit world, the divine, universal energy, angels, and spirit guides interchangeably. They are all a part of a greater source representing divine love and oneness. And it is within this universal spirit that we are all interconnected.

CHAPTER 1

When Time Stands Still

Have you ever had one of those moments when time stands still? When the workings of your mind seem to defy time and space, and you are able to connect on a soul level to a loved one from a distance?

This phenomenon has always existed. There are many documented cases where divine timing is at work whether it is deja vu, a knowing, a premonition or an overwhelming urge to phone a family member in need. Many refer to these synchronistic moments in life as coincidences or divine interventions. However, these synchronicities are a much deeper connection of being one with God. These time warps are a glimpse into the sheer magnitude of our lives and our infinite connection to each other.

I have been blessed with many synchronicities in life, whether I understood them all at the time or not. Oftentimes, my moments of clarity did not occur until years after the fact, as I started to piece together the workings of my soul. There have also been a few life-defining moments that opened my eyes to the universal connection within us all. Moments that instantly confirmed there is a greater force at work and left me yearning for more.

My greatest spiritual awakening moment (so far) occurred when I was in my early twenties. To this day, I cannot remember what happened before or after the event. However, I assure you, it was average, standard issue, young, and carefree stuff. I was living away from home for the first time, enjoying my newfound freedom, my first job out of university, and my active nightlife. I was not involved in any spiritual growth or religious pursuits. Life was good, and I was simply enjoying the ride.

Then it happened. One night in the middle of a peaceful sleep I was gently awakened by an angel. A very real, loving, and calming spiritual being sent to me by God with a specific yet gentle message. "Your mom has just gone into cardiac arrest. Wake up and pray for her. Send her healing energies. Let her know that she is loved and needed."

That night, without questioning who this being was, why my healthy young mom would be in danger or if I would even make any difference at all...I prayed. I prayed with all my heart and soul. I sent love, light, and healing energies to my mom; I cried and asked her to stay. In my mind's eye I saw an emergency room where my mom was at the centre of attention as she lay in peaceful distress, her heart flat-lining. All of this, I did from over 100km away.

I continued to pray for my mom and sent her healing energies (certainly new terminology and experiences for me at the time, by the way). Then the angel spoke again. "Your mom is okay now. Go back to sleep." And again, without question, I peacefully laid back down, closed my eyes, and instantly dozed off. Not for one minute did I question what happened. It was a magical moment and I certainly felt blessed.

Until the morning came that is. When I woke, I started to doubt myself about what had occurred the night before. I was even embarrassed by my reaction and what clearly must have been an overactive imagination. Why would I even think my mom would have been in distress? And then of course the bigger question, who was I to think a messenger of God would ask me to pray and help heal someone's health? Sure, I was young and full of zest and confidence... but help to heal another individual, who the hell did I think I was?

This thought process went on for about an hour. Then there was that clarifying moment that forever changed my life...the phone rang. "Everything is okay," my dad said, "but, last night, your mom went into cardiac arrest. It was a code blue and then she was resuscitated. The doctors have her stabilized now and she is doing fine."

Fast-forward nearly twenty years. As eye-opening, miraculous, and blessed as that event may have been, I spent much of my earlier years moving on, pretending like that night never happened. I blocked out further contact and mystical experiences from the other side. I pursued different interests that were more mainstream to society, and that would not subject my family or myself to judgment and ridicule.

However, despite my efforts to bury the event in the past, these experiences continued to happen until it came to the point I could no longer ignore my spiritual encounters. After years of denial, I finally started to acknowledge my truths and worked to understand what had transpired that magical night.

The base line for my entire SOULworks has and always will be this one miraculous moment with my mom. The events surrounding that night will always be in my heart. Looking back, what I found to be most liberating about the experience was the realization that while submerged in the actual event, I had jumped right in with both feet and never questioned the power within.

On the other hand, once my mind had a chance to digest what had happened, my inner light began to dim and was replaced with self-doubt, questions, and disbelief. I started to dismiss my truths and went back to my old, clouded way of thinking. Why do we as a society, so often dismiss the unknown? Why do we lack confidence in our abilities? I have spent much of my life trying to get back to the inner peace and strength I felt that night, to feel confident in myself and my God-given potential. It has been a long journey. The path to our SOULworks is not any easy one.

Activating your SOULworks

When I look back over the events of that miraculous night, I still cannot completely explain why I stayed quiet about my experience for so long. I was visited by an angel, clearly shown accurate details of a situation transpiring miles away, was asked to help by sending healing energies, and was even given confirmation within hours of the occurrence. And yet, there was a larger part of me still doubtful. A larger part scared to admit what had taken place. It would not be until years later, I felt brave enough and armed with enough information and experiences to speak my truth. This reality makes me very sad.

Imagine how different our world would be if everyone was open and honest about spiritual encounters. Imagine how peaceful and serene our lives could be if we all learned to listen to our spirit guides and always responded when asked. Picture how blessed our reality would be if we only opened our minds and hearts to the unknown. How miraculous our existence if we believed in miracles today, as much as those who walked the earth before us. Suppose no one criticized others for speaking their truth. Imagine in the power of faith. Just imagine.

Perhaps it is just me. Maybe I am the only one out there who has been scared to speak up and discuss topics our world is so quick to dismiss. Perhaps I am the only one who awkwardly stands in the New Age section of the bookstore seeking answers, and desperately hoping no one I know walks by. Unfortunately, I do not think that is the case.

The term *New Age* has been defined as a broad movement of alternative approaches to traditional culture, with an interest in spirituality, mysticism, the paranormal, and oneness. Sure, it sounds scary at first, but I have grown to love the New Age movement, and have personally found it to be very uplifting. In fact, upon closer inspection the New Age movement is not really so new at all. There are many cultures around the world that have practiced spiritual growth, enlightenment, healing, energy work, channelling of messages, and divinely inspired prophecies since the beginning of time.

I started my New Age journey scared, alone, and feeling like I was on a dimly lit road that was evil and forbidden to be travelled. However, once I faced my fears and delved into the unknown, I found it to be full of enlightenment, beauty, and truth (and even a lot of really nice people). Although this road may still be less travelled, I would suggest that the path has always been there. Some of us may have just forgotten the way.

Your Move:

- ❑ **Expand your mind.** Have you visited the New Age section of a bookstore lately? You probably have because this book successfully crossed your path. So first off, give yourself a pat on the back for striving to enhance your spiritual awareness. I encourage you to keep an open mind while reading about my experiences, and then challenge yourself to further expand your own awareness to the unknown. The demand and thirst for spiritual and New Age materials has literally burst onto the scene over the last twenty years. When I first encountered the spirit world, there were little to no resources on the subject matter. At the time, if you found a handful of books you would consider yourself lucky. I have watched this section slowly grow over time from one row of shelves to numerous. Our society craves this information and the demand is evident. People are looking for answers and desire to increase their awareness.

Never cease to expand your mind. There is always more to learn. Continue to push yourself as you grow. Leave your old narrow ways of thinking behind. Embrace the future and the spiritual age of evolution.

❑ **Appreciate moments with the divine.** I do not actually remember ever thanking the angels for including me along the journey of that miraculous night with my mom. Please learn to always show gratitude for your connection with spirit, no matter what the size of the encounter. Acknowledge you are not alone in this world, and appreciate the divine glimpses of heaven that occur everyday. The setting of the sun, birds singing in the trees, moments you feel vulnerable and alone, every breath of everyday, you are one with spirit.

❑ **Speak your truth.** Stand up for your beliefs. Express your spiritual experiences. Do not be afraid to demonstrate your faith to the world. This has become a lost art. The world has focused all our efforts in arguing which religion bears the most truth. In this, we have forgotten the most important part. The best spiritual practice for any one person is the practice that brings them closest to spirit. This can be done anywhere. The important part is to express your faith in the spirit world, believe in the unknown, understand your connection with the divine, and speak your truth.

❑ **Share your energy.** Divine energy is always abundant and free flowing. It resides in and around you infinitely at a soul level. Utilize your free will to tap into and use this life force whenever you feel guided. Send energetic hugs to those who need your help. Envision the light of the world filling up your entire life: past, present, and future, blessing you and all who cross your path. Share the energy you have freely for there is always more. Imagine yourself and others becoming lighter and lighter with this divine vibrational energy. Believe your efforts are making a difference. For they truly are.

CHAPTER 2

Hope Conquers All

This story is about hope. Hope is one of the largest obstacles I have had to overcome in my healing practice. It is not so much that I did not always have a strong belief and hope system for myself. My issue stemmed from a fear of giving hope to others. It has taken many experiences and lessons to get to the point where I do not fear or worry about spreading hope. Here is where it all started.

One morning as I woke up from a deep sleep, my deceased grandpa greeted me. He was standing by my bedside requesting I pass on a message to my dad. "Tell your dad he does not have to worry about his health. Everything will be okay and it is not his time to go home (to heaven)."

As I slowly started to comprehend the encounter that had just occurred, I rubbed the sleep from my eyes and double-checked my memory banks. Dad had never expressed or discussed any health problems. I had also not heard from my grandpa in many years. Why had he come to me now, and to what health issue was he referring? Should I actually approach my dad with this information? I was imaging a scenario in my mind where dad was not worried about his health until I mentioned my vision, and then he started to worry. For this reason, I was afraid to talk to dad, and instead kept the message of hope to myself.

About two weeks later my mom and dad came for a visit. While there, they broke the news; dad had been diagnosed with cancer. We were all heart broken and concerned for his well-being. Of course, I immediately remembered the message of hope from grandpa and was trying to get up the courage to deliver it. During this time of my life, I was still very closed off to my family about my experiences and conversations with the other side. As everyone in the room continued to talk, I drifted off from the conversation and began to plan my speech. I imagined it would go something like, "so, funny thing happened the other day. You know your dad, the one that has been dead for 25 years? Well he stopped by...."

From my thoughts, I was jolted back into the room by my dad's conversation and mounting anxiety level. He was sharing with the family all the different medical treatment options that were available. Dad was incredibly stressed by his new reality and was having trouble deciding which avenue to take. The unknown scared him so much. With his mounting fear and anxiety level, mine too began to escalate. My apprehension of sharing the message of hope kicked into high gear and with it my speech flew right out the window. What would happen if I told dad grandpa's message? Would it change dad's decision on which treatment to pursue? Would this change affect the intended outcome and grandpa's message of hope? I stayed silent once again. There would be no message of hope delivered that day.

In fact, I never did deliver that message of hope during his illness. My dad eventually pursued a few cancer treatment options and was able to fight the disease. Grandpa was right; it was not his time to go home. All was well in my dad's world once again. Even so, I have always regretted not having the confidence to pass on the message when I was asked. The hope was there to make a very stressful situation into one that could have been far easier on my dad. I was given the opportunity to make a difference in someone's life and I was too scared to take action. This encounter would be one of the many great lessons in my life. Filled with regret and disappointment in myself, I vowed to take action if ever presented with a similar opportunity. Next time I would not be afraid to speak up and give someone a message of hope. But would spirit trust me enough to provide another chance?

Turns out I would be given many opportunities within my life to pass on messages of hope. What I have also since learned from having more experience in this field and watching spirit work in wondrous ways, is the simple fact that everything happens for a reason and everything happens in its time. When it is not a person's time to go, it is not their time to go. This decision is made on a soul level. And although we may not always be consciously aware of the outcome – once the decision is made to stay, our bodies will respond and recover. From that perspective, it would not have mattered what treatment decision my dad made, the outcome would have been the same...my dad was destined to be a cancer survivor.

I have also learned another aspect about hope even for those whose time has come. Never ever be afraid to give someone hope even in their final moments here on earth. Hope is what makes our spirits soar. Hope is what brings light into our lives and brings us closer to God. And it is within that magical moment, hope bridges heaven and earth, enabling our soul to reach its destiny and continue the journey. Wherever that journey may be.

Activating your SOULworks

Our spirit guides and departed loved ones often seek to communicate in the wee hours of the morning just as we are waking from a night of slumber. My grandpa and many others have chosen this method to get my attention over the years. This is because our logical minds have yet to kick into high gear and our hearts are still within our dream world. It is during this lucid state we are substantially more open to hear, see or feel their interactions. The same concept is true when in a full dream state, although in this case symbolism is more frequently utilized, and our imaginations activated within the message.

The actual messages conveyed vary depending on what is going on in our lives. Sometimes spirit communicates to provide insights, support, guidance, and hope. At other times, we are forewarned of danger, given glimpses of potential future events, and urged to heed caution. It still never ceases to amaze me how we humans find it so hard to accept messages of hope and love. However, send us a message of pending doom, and we are much quicker to respond. Unfortunately, it usually takes the threat of impending danger to get our attention and motivate us into action. Are you the exception to this rule or the norm?

Your Move:

- ❑ **Give hope abundantly.** Hope is the expectation or promise of a positive outcome. Hope is playing the part of an optimist instead of a pessimist. Hope is to a dream like water is to a seed; it is integral to manifesting a positive future. Start having a more positive outlook on your life and the lives of others. Do not be afraid to let people believe in miracles, even those who are terminally ill. Imagine the outcome as a success and then watch your spirit grow.

- ❑ **Receive hope graciously.** To heal is to accept hope into your life with grace and ease. When you open your heart to hope, you are opening your energy field to receive blessings from the divine. When someone sends positive vibes your direction, please accept them with open arms. Do not be the naysayer who insists nothing will ever change. Receive the gift of hope as easily and gratefully as you would a compliment. Give thanks for these positive words or blessings, and believe an encouraging outcome will arrive.

❏ **Re-evaluate your largest struggles.** Take a closer look at all the elements in your life you believe are a struggle. For some it may be weight issues, for others financial concerns, still others struggle with health and well-being; it does not really matter where the resistance lies. What we are looking for are the elements in your life where you have lost all hope in changing. The hardships you feel that are just destined to be. Ask yourself what lessons you have learned from these hardships. Then give your concerns to your angels and declare you are no longer controlled by these struggles. Give yourself permission to give your hopeless situations a good dowsing of hope. Send light towards each struggle and visualize it no longer being an obstacle in your life. Expect a positive outcome. Receive change.

❏ **Send hope to Mother Earth.** So many people believe our world is in danger. There are countless theories of doom, global warming, environmental catastrophes, wide spread disease, famine, and war. Certainly there is cause for concern, for society has not been kind to Mother Earth. However, there is also cause for optimism and hope. The struggles of our world have already been identified; there is no need to dwell on the negative. In fact, to do so would be detrimental. Begin to send our world hope. Raise the bar for your expectations of a positive outcome. Become more active in making constructive changes, and send uplifting energies across the globe. Hope, light, and love will change our world.

CHAPTER 3

In Times of Need

For the first three decades of my life I did not really have a clear understanding of my abilities. I certainly remembered being asked to channel energies for my mom. However, besides that one special experience, all other information I received had consisted of small tidbits of information or premonitions that were not always clear and concise. And for that very reason, I always assumed helping to heal my mom had been a once in a life time occurrence; a chance happening with the divine never to be repeated.

Wow, was I wrong. Looking back, I can clearly see the experience was not a one-time event, but the start of a life-long journey of healing. Nearly twenty years after my first experience, my angelic radar clearly and accurately sounded once again. A second family member was in distress, and I was asked by spirit to step up to the plate and help out. Once again, I did so without question...well, sort of.

My family had just received a very happy phone call notifying us of a new addition to our family. We were celebrating for my younger brother and his wife who were now the proud parents of a baby boy.

Everyone was very excited. A new life into the world always brings so much joy.

At the time of the birth, my brother had indicated everyone was doing fine, and that both mom and baby were resting. I remember him clearly saying all is well, but please give us time to catch up on our sleep before coming to the hospital for a visit. The labor had been incredibly long and everyone was so very tired.

In any normal circumstance, their request would have been very reasonable and appropriate. However, I could not get over the feeling something was very wrong. In the back of my mind, my spirit guides were asking me to get to the hospital and provide some sort of support. I struggled with the two different versions of the story. On one hand, I was hearing from my brother all was fine. On the other hand, the situation was quite different. Although I did not understand what the problem was exactly, I was most certainly receiving strong guidance to go to the hospital and help.

At this point, I really wanted to honor my brother and sister-in-law's wishes. They had clearly requested we give them space, and I was confident they did not want to have any company. Besides, if something were wrong, would they not have said?

I even tried bargaining with my spirit guides. I actually pointed out that during my mom's experience I successfully sent healing energies from the comfort of my home over 100km away; surely, I could send healing energies at a much shorter distance. Besides, the baby was such a little guy, how could he possibly need a lot of energetic support so early on in life?

Regardless of what I tried to tell myself, the urges persisted to no avail. The instructions to go to the hospital and send healing energies continuously ran through my mind. I felt completely off balance the entire day and I was having trouble determining my course of action. I even told my husband I did not want to continue with our original plans to have a fun outing that day. I adamantly felt something was wrong with the baby, and I should stay within reach so I could provide support.

Although no one understood my concerns, my husband and two children did agree to leave me at home to pace the floor, as they continued on with their day. No sooner had they left our house when the phone rang. My suspicions had finally been confirmed. My mom was on the other line. She was very distraught and upset as she recounted the story. Earlier that day, mom had gone to visit her new grandson. While there, the hospital staff noticed the newborn baby was non-responsive on the right side. After tests were completed it was determined the baby had suffered a stroke during labor. My mom urged me to go to the hospital and provide comfort as she continued to contact family, spread the news, and request their support in prayers.

Unfortunately, it took this confirmation phone call to get me moving, but once the information was received, I was in the car and on my way to the hospital. My suspicions had finally been defined. It was not a good feeling, but I finally knew without a doubt my apprehensions throughout the day had been for a reason, and I was needed in some way. In what way exactly, was still a very large mystery to me. While speeding towards the hospital, I started asking my guides for help on how to proceed. I was told very clearly to send healing energies to the baby, surround him with good thoughts, and to give hope to his concerned and overwhelmed parents.

Since I was still very aware my brother and sister-in-law were not feeling up to having visitors, my first line of business was with the baby. I used my intuition and swiftly moved through the hospital to find approximately where he was located. Then, because I was still unsure and insecure about what I was doing within the healing process, I literally hid myself near the baby and started to channel energy. The situation felt very similar to when my mom was in the hospital. Even though I was not in the room with my little nephew, I could see the baby's location in my mind's eye and visualize where the energy needed to go. I even started to enhance my abilities by calling upon Archangel Raphael to help guide the process. I sent green healing energies to surround the baby and cocooned him in a protective layer of love and support. These visualizations were new to me and I questioned where the ideas came from. Who was this Archangel Raphael? Why would I be calling upon him? And why was I visualizing this beautiful emerald green energy? At the time, the answers did not really matter, but I did tuck these questions into the back of my mind and then continued with the task at hand. Instinctively I continued to send energy, I prayed for support, and sent that little guy all the love I could muster.

About an hour had passed when I heard from my angels again. They indicated it was time to visit the new parents and give them hope. Receiving a request to pass on a message of hope was not a new experience for me; as mentioned, my angels had made similar requests in the past. However, never had I actually responded nor spoken up to tell someone everything was going to be okay. Even the thought of approaching my brother made me feel vulnerable and out of my comfort zone. And besides, who was I to know what the results would be? What if I was wrong? What if I provided them with false hopes?

These questions did not last for very long, for I began to be moved by a force far greater than me. Very quickly I made my way through the hospital and found myself standing outside of the gift shop. Upon entering the store, I was immediately drawn to an area in the back that seemed to just light up. On the shelf was a collection of angel pins, and the very first one that caught my attention was called the *Angel of Hope*. Tears streamed down my face, as I quickly purchased the little angel and then headed up to the room.

When I knocked on the door and entered, I could see the reaction in both parents' eyes. They were devastated by the news received earlier that day and would have really preferred to be by themselves to digest their new reality. I quickly gave my brother a hug and assured him I was not staying long. I said I was there to let them know everything would be okay. I even went on to say they would take the baby home with them on Wednesday and that all would be fine. Even as I was saying the words, I was thinking to myself where is this coming from? Why would I so clearly state information for something so unknown?

My brother was equally perplexed. He said he appreciated my positive outlook and for trying to provide hope, but they had just heard from the doctor the baby was not doing well at all, and in fact may never come home. As my brother spoke of the harsh reality, I was completely speechless but my mind was whirling. Why in the world had my guides sent me here to give hope to what seemed a hopeless situation? Why had I spouted off a message that was so darn specific? Did I really just guarantee a release from the hospital on Wednesday? What in the world was I thinking? On that awkward note, I gave my brother another hug, handed him the angel pin of hope, said my goodbyes, and left the room.

I did not actually leave though. I spent the rest of the day still hiding in the hospital, sending healing energies to the baby. I could not even explain why. I was completely embarrassed and horrified by the exchange that had transpired with my brother, and yet forces greater than me were once again keeping my body hostage. Despite the hesitations I had as a person, my inner self stayed strong and I did not give up. I provided the support my spiritual guides requested of me, even though I so clearly did not understand the scope of my work.

Time flew by without me even realizing. Then all of a sudden, I heard within my mind, it was time to go to the cafeteria. Without questioning why I was following this inner guidance, I got up and was on the move to the other end of the hospital. It is there that I ran into my brother who was having supper with my dad. I think I was more surprised to see them, then they were to see me. I had been there all day and yet decided at that exact moment it was time to move locations. They both asked what I was still doing there. Had I really been there all day? I did not even know how to answer the question. I could hardly believe it myself. I had been so engrossed in sending healing energy that I had not even noticed how much time had passed. Besides, how could I begin to explain this inner need to send healing energy when truthfully, I knew very little about it? Despite my vague answer to their question, which I cannot even remember to this day, we had a good talk and I felt a little better about what had transpired.

When I finally left the hospital, I did not go home. Instead, I went to the local bookstore in search of a frame of reference or explanation for the day's experiences. I was guided to an area in the store, then an aisle, and then a book. It practically jumped right off the shelf at me. I quickly ran home and began to read. In there, I found references to Archangel Raphael and it was noted he is known for his healing abilities. The book went on to further account for the emerald green I had used earlier that day, and described it as a color that has been attributed to healing since the beginning of time. I was both relieved and perplexed. How did I know this information prior to reading the book? How could it be that I have so much knowledge in the area of healing that is only now beginning to surface? I began to feel more confident about the day's events and convinced a healing was in fact taking place. I even started to be more hopeful on Wednesday's discharge from the hospital and was pleased with the progress.

Unfortunately, Wednesday came and Wednesday went, and the baby was still in intensive care. It had even been determined he was having seizures, with upwards of 25 a day. The entire family was devastated. I too felt bad for my brother and his family, but mostly I was disappointed in my guides and myself. I even yelled at my angelic team that day. "Why work through me and put me through this emotional roller coaster if it does not make a difference? What good is hope if it does not deliver some sort of reprieve?" I demanded. Their answer was the same as it had always been, "continue to send healing energies, and continue to trust in the divine order within this situation." I cried a lot that day and then worked to pull myself together; not for me, but for my nephew.

Even with my pride broken from being wrong about the discharge date of Wednesday, I did not give up. I actually took a few days off work and continued to send healing energies. I could not explain why I was being asked to help, but it was very evident to me that I was certainly being asked. I read more books, learned more about the guidance I was receiving, and continued to send positive light and love to my brother's baby boy. And on the following Wednesday, he was released from the hospital and went home with his parents... thanks be to God.

It was that very day I looked up to the heavens and gave thanks where thanks were certainly due. I also for the first time in my life, realized how I wanted to dedicate my life to whatever this was that was going on within me. I still had so many questions, so much to learn, and so many experiences to encounter. However, I knew with all my heart that if I could help someone move forward in his or her life in some way, I would do everything I could to make that happen. If my guides were asking me to step in and have the courage to speak up and show that we as individuals can make a difference in someone's life, then that is what I would certainly strive to do.

My nephew has grown to be a wonderfully healthy and active child despite original expectations of doctors and family. He has defied all odds, conquered so many obstacles, and demonstrated to our family the power of prayer, hope, and courage. He is the most wonderful little angel I have ever seen, and I am so grateful to have been able to contribute to his life and him to mine. Thank you to my wonderful nephew who blessed me with this experience. I am forever grateful that you gave me the opportunity to find and let my light shine.

Activating your SOULworks

We live in a world where our spiritual connections are often dismissed. For the most part, our society believes we are alone in this world, left to struggle through whatever life throws our way; that life is cruel and our impact on each other's lives is futile. I strongly disagree.

What I have learned from my nephew is that our powerful souls are capable of contributing to extraordinary miracles, so long as our earthly minds get out of the way for our true spirit to shine. I have also learned these life-defining moments do not have to be so few and far between as I had originally believed. We can always live in unison with the universe and those we love. We do hold the power within to help facilitate a healing. We are connected to the divine light and have access to utilize this energy whenever needed. The connection is there and readily available for us to utilize. We just have to be aware of and learn how to tap into this energy. Likewise, it is possible to lift the veil between our worlds, follow our inner guidance, and flow with the energies of the universe. We only need to open our hearts, minds, and souls to allow the experience in.

If there is anything you learn from this book, please understand we all have the ability to positively impact our lives and the lives of those around us.

Your Move:

- ❑ **Activate the healer within.** To activate your God-given healing powers, you only need to hold the intention to do so and believe. Understand you have access to this universal energy at all times. Choose someone in your life to send energy to. This can be a friend in need, a family member or even yourself. Use your imagination and visualize your spirit moving upwards towards the heavens. From this vantage point you will become closer to the universal energy and may find it easier to see within your mind's eye your intended target. Picture the person within your mind. Use your intuition to select a color that feels right, and visualize this color of light moving from the heavens towards the person in need. Surround them in this healing force. Envision all health problems shifting to their optimum state. Believe.

- ❑ **Trust in your abilities.** Never doubt for one moment you are helping to facilitate a positive change. Remove your fears from the situation and trust in the divine order of all things. Any love and energy that you send people is always beneficial. It creates positive changes for all involved and does impact their lives. Appreciate the power you all hold to create a positive outcome and strive to harness this dormant power. It is there for you to utilize. Let your light shine.

- ❑ **Create a prayer box.** A prayer box is a simple way to send love and light to a number of people in a timely and effective manner. Write the names of all those you hold near and dear to your heart on small slips of paper. Then fold the paper and place each name within a special box. Hold the intention for positive energy to freely flow to all the names contained within. Develop a routine to tune in and send good vibes to everyone on a daily basis.

❑ **Ask and respond.** Take a more active role in sending positive energy towards those in need. You can utilize your intuition for this task by letting your inner self guide you to the person who requires an extra boost of energy. Trust in the answer you receive. Another option is to use your prayer box to select the person requiring an energetic lift. Ask your guides to provide the name of a loved one who is in need of a healing today, and then reach into the box to select a piece of paper. Trust the name you receive and send them an extra dose of love that day. Take the time to send good thoughts towards the person. There is no need to understand the entire situation or receive all the details before taking action. Simply ask, watch or listen for the answer, and then activate the light within.

CHAPTER 4

Back to the Light

This next story begins with the launch of my business - SOULworks. I had just nicely reached a point in my life where I felt confident in my abilities. I had even started to open up to family and friends about my personal encounters with the spirit world. Progress was being made as I studied in the field of spiritualism, defined the scope of my work, and narrowed my focus on providing a service of Intuitive Healing. It may have taken a very long time to move forward along my spiritual path, but once I made the decision to change my life and speak my truth, everything started to come together very quickly. I clearly declared on my new website my encounters with the spirit world. I confidently proclaimed how I interact with the angels, strive to respond to their guidance, and answer their requests to help those in need. I even had business cards printed. Life was good. In fact, for the first time ever, I felt I was on track and doing the work I was truly meant to do. I took pride in having made it this far, not only recognizing when my angels and guides were communicating with me, but more importantly, finally starting to listen and respond to them when asked.

My earlier career in marketing and communications was also very successful at this time. Although I was slowly beginning to transition out of this line of work, I had recently won a number of national awards for my efforts in marketing and public relations and was on my way to Banff, Alberta, Canada to receive recognition at an awards banquet. I will say it again: life was very good.

A few days after my SOULworks business was launched, I was talking on the phone with a family member. She was sharing some very good news. My cousin Lyndon, who had been experiencing severe depression, was finally seeing improvements in his life. He had moved back home to be with family and seemed very content with sharing time with his loved ones. Everyone was very excited with his progress and was thankful for his change in demeanor.

Talking to my relative, I could feel her joy and yet my angelic radar was going off again. Two different messages were coming through. There was the joy and relief I clearly felt from my family members; there was also the apprehension and uncertainty I instinctively felt around Lyndon. I said nothing.

When I got off the phone, I tried to tap into Lyndon's energy field to see if my suspicions were correct and to send him healing energy. Over the years, I had learned that I could zoom into someone at a soul level, ask if they wanted to receive healing, and then channel energy just as I had done so many years ago with my mom. However, this situation was different. It was like nothing I had ever experienced before. As I tried to zoom into Lyndon's energy field, I felt like I had hit a brick wall. His response to my question of offering help was a resounding no, and I truly felt like I was being blocked from sending healing energy his way. I had read about other healers having experienced similar responses when an individual is not ready to be helped, but I had never truly experienced this sensation before. At the time, I respected Lyndon's response without fully realizing the scope of the situation or my decision to back away. I did not push the healing any further; I just moved on with my own life and busy schedule.

As I drove into town later that day, I passed a spot along the road that sent chills down my spine. It was like I entered a time warp and within it I heard myself talking on the phone. The conversation started with my mom saying she had some very bad news about Lyndon. Then as quickly as it had started, I drove out of the zone and heard no more. I wondered if the vision had any validity or if I was just being paranoid from the events earlier that morning. What could the bad news possibly have been? In the end, I decided I was just paranoid. A decision I would later regret with my whole heart.

Another premonition regarding Lyndon came the day before I was to leave for Banff for the awards ceremony. I was in a rush and driving to work so I could pick up a few things from the office. When I reached the same place in the road, time once again stood still. I heard an urgent voice in my mind pleading for me to pull over and contact Lyndon immediately, for he desperately needed my help. My thought process was garbled. What would I say? I had not talked to Lyndon in literally years. Would he think I was crazy to offer my support? What support was I going to provide? What if I was wrong? Would my talk of visions, spirits, and expressing my concerns make his situation worse? I had never even discussed or shared my spiritual experiences with Lyndon. How would he respond? Eventually, I just talked myself out of it. There I was in a hurry to get to work so I could pack for my trip. I vowed to myself with the intention of definitely following through with a call to Lyndon straight away on Monday morning upon my return. He had been in trouble before in his life, surely he could wait a few more days. With that final thought, I dismissed the entire occurrence and moved on with my own agenda.

The following day as I headed to the airport, I received the official call from my mom just as we were driving through that all too familiar stretch of road. The conversation started just as I had predicted, with my mom saying she had some bad news about Lyndon. He had been found dead in his home and the police were investigating. As more information was later revealed, it was determined Lyndon had taken his own life. His time of death was exactly one hour after I had received the urgent plea to contact him the day before.

I will forever be sorry for not reaching out to Lyndon. I review those last two weeks of his life over and over and over in my mind. I know without a doubt I should have had the guts to pick up the phone. Spirit had reached out to me to help a child of God, my cousin, and a dear friend to many, and I literally said I was too scared and busy. What kind of a world do we live in when I am too self-absorbed to help a person in need? I do not know what I would have said or if I could have made a difference at all, but a person should never ever be afraid to reach out and lend a helping hand to anyone, even if the source of information is unclear or vague.

It is true that I never fully understood the scope of what Lyndon was going through nor did I suspect my dear young cousin would take his own life. However, I should not have needed the full front-page story before I would agree to intervene. Ironically, I had felt completely prepared to open my business and expand my reach only days earlier, and yet when I was called into action my fears still stopped me. I was too worried about what people would think of my actions, instead of focusing my attention on why Lyndon would need my help in the first place. I gave my ego priority and I was wrong. I should have stepped up to the plate and strived to make a difference, to be the bigger person that I know I can be. But I didn't, and unfortunately, I cannot change my mistakes. Trust me, I have tried.

To both Lyndon and his family, I am truly sorry. It has been a hard lesson and heartbreaking experience I will certainly remember forever. Lyndon was an incredibly gifted old soul who held wisdom and knowledge beyond his years. He helped so many friends and family in need, and positively impacted the lives of many. He just never had the chance to fully understand his own gifts and potential. In a journal entry Lyndon made during some of his darkest days, he indicated, "All I need is to get back to what I already have inside me." These insights are so profound and important for everyone to hear, so listen up. Somewhere deep inside we are all a spark of divine light. We are all one with God, capable of tuning into our sixth senses and accessing our soul potential. And yet, to this day most of us do not. The path to our SOULworks is not an easy one. In memory of Lyndon, please know we are all capable of extraordinary lives that have the potential to mimic heaven here on earth. Please take the time to find your inner light and let it shine; you are so worth it.

To my dear friend Lyndon, Spirit is so very lucky to have such a wonderful person back home. As sure as I know our souls live on forever, I also know you are successfully carrying on your life journey, reaching out and touching the hearts of many forever and ever. I vow to follow in your footsteps, and strive to do the same.

Activating your SOULworks

Becoming enlightened and more open to spirit has enhanced my life, my blessings, and my understanding of the ways of the world. I cherish every moment communicating with spirit and would never regret my increased awareness. What I do regret are all the times in my life I have not acted upon the advice of spirit. The moments I misunderstood the information or dismissed the guidance provided entirely because of pride and fear. As I become more aware of my surroundings, I also become more aware of the abilities I have within myself to facilitate positive change. Not responding to these moments of divine knowledge can be heartbreaking.

I believe learning to always follow our intuition is key. If we were taught at an early age to pursue our gut feelings, listen to our guides, hear the energetic cries of those in need, and respond without question, our world would be a far better place. This is the goal I strive to teach others and myself: to never dismiss the voice within our heart.

Until this greatness is achieved, forgiveness is a powerful tool. It has the ability to heal our hearts, our minds, and our souls. When forgiveness is not given, it also has the ability to tear our hearts apart, devastate our minds, affect our health, and wound our souls. Choose forgiveness. There are going to be many times in our lives when we need to stop beating ourselves up about the mistakes we have made, and forgive ourselves for the outcome. Recognize we are all still human here on earth having a human experience. Our souls may live on forever, but while here on earth, we do not always hear and listen to its eternal wisdom. Forgiveness is the only way to fully accept the lessons learned, and to move forward from an overwhelming experience. To forgive is to heal.

Your Move:

- ❑ **Embrace your divine wisdom.** Begin to pay close attention to your own inner knowing. You are connected to the universal knowledge of spirit and have the ability to access this information at any time. Become conscious of what information you pick up on, whether it is for a person, place or thing. Do you like the energy? How does it make you feel? Can you sense when someone is upset or something is wrong? How do you receive this information? Is it a gut feeling, a knowing, guidance from your higher self, an image within your mind's eye, a bad taste in your mouth or does something just smell funny to you? Do not be afraid to take the time and really tune into a situation. Ask your guides what you need to know, and if there is anything you can do to help create a more positive outcome.

❑ **Pick yourself up.** Learn from the lessons life throws your way. It is within your darkest days and largest challenges, when you have the opportunity to move forward by leaps and bounds. Thank spirit for the lessons learned, and recognize your soul will grow and develop from this experience. Make a list of all the many challenges in your life for which you are still unsettled. Look for the hidden lessons beneath the heartache. Acknowledge the soul lessons provided by your family, your situation, your misguided endeavors, and your blessings. Give thanks for the lessons learned and turn the situation over to your guides and angels. Trust you are exactly where you need to be and ask spirit to always accompany you on your journey.

❑ **Forgive and forget.** You cannot fully live in the present if you spend all your time harboring past resentments and regrets. Let your soul move forward along its path. Gracefully forgive all experiences in all directions of time that are no longer serving you to your highest good. For those whose lives are troubled, forgive yourself for the situations you are in and the path you have chosen to follow. For families whose hearts are shattered from the life choices of others, learn to honor their paths, understand their struggles, and accept their decisions. Embrace your loved ones for who they are. Send them light and love, trusting they are always being watched over and cared for.

❑ **Create change.** If you do not like the way things are going in your life or decisions you have made in the past, make an effort to shift your focus and change your direction. Do not spend any time wallowing in self-pity; to do so is self-destructive. Instead, consciously put positive thoughts into your preferred outcome and accept this change as your new truth. For example, if you are suffering from depression, start visualizing yourself as a happy and content person. Then go out and do something fun and interesting that makes you happy. While in this state of bliss, thank spirit for this blessing and ask to have many more of these experiences brought your way. Trust this outcome is manifesting. Use your intentions to help bring this truth into being.

CHAPTER 5

The Bird Lady

I have always had a fascination with birds. I love to hear them sing, watch them soar above, and observe the different types of birds as they each bring peaceful serenity to their surrounding environment. During the first part of my life, my relationship with this beautiful species was fairly general and for the most part uneventful.

Around the time I turned thirty-five however, a new relationship with birds started to unfold. In particular, a specific event changed my perspective on birds and the role they play in our lives. In fact, my newfound friends literally changed the way I viewed the animal kingdom and their interactions with our soul path.

It was two weeks prior to my younger brother's wedding and I was at my in-laws for a family picnic. The ladies were sitting outside on the patio enjoying a beautiful day of sunshine, cool beverages, and visiting. During the afternoon, the topic of my brother's wedding was brought up, and I joyfully shared with my husband's side of the family, details about the wonderful bride my brother was about to marry and the wedding plans that were well underway.

At the end of our conversation I drifted off in my mind and silently voiced to myself how I wished my grandparents had lived long enough to see my brother get married. You see, he was the youngest in the family and my grandparents were always voicing their concerns, pressuring him to find a girl and settle down while they were still around and able to attend the wedding (talk about putting on the pressure). Even with all their teasing, my brother was always a good sport, and I am sure he would have loved to comply with their wishes had the timing been right. Unfortunately, they all crossed over to the spirit world prior to his big day.

As my mind wandered, I became slowly aware of something that had gently landed on my hand, and although I was starting to move my eyes toward that direction, I was also being prompted to listen to the whisper of spirit. At this point, I looked down and realized a bird was sitting on my hand. A simple little chickadee was sitting there and telepathically speaking to me, in what sounded like my deceased grandpa's voice. His message was clear "watch for us, we will be there." I sat there with a mesmerized look on my face. I was not frightened by the bird sitting on my hand, only fascinated by the sheer magnitude of the small visitor and the message I had just received.

At that point, and of course not realizing what had just transpired between the bird and myself, my family began laughing. After all, it is not every day a bird lands on your hand while sitting around in a group of people. The laughs were quickly followed by the bird's departure. As gracefully as the bird had entered my life, it gracefully flew away. Everyone teased and suggested I had been sitting in one place for far too long. Why else would a bird sit on my hand? The little chickadee must have thought I was a tree, my in-laws joked. I laughed along with the group but did not dismiss what had just transpired. I knew a message had been sent to me through my winged friend, and I was honored to have received the message.

The wedding day quickly arrived and it was yet another beautiful day. The ceremony was outdoors in the most perfect setting with trees, gardens, and loved ones all around. I was cozily seated in the middle of a row and surrounded by people on all four sides, as I watched the ceremony unfold. Everything was perfect and I had never seen my brother look so happy. To be honest, I was so absorbed in the day's events I had almost forgotten about the message I received two weeks prior. But at the end of the ceremony, and right on cue, as the minister announced, "I now pronounce you man and wife," a bird flew down through the crowd and literally grazed my cheek to get my attention. I could actually feel the warm gentle feathered wings, as they glided over my face. I then watched in sheer awe, as the bird flew up above the crowd and joined five other feathered friends directly above my brother and his new wife. It was like something straight out of a Disney movie. The music started to play and the group began to cheer, as the special union was finalized. All eyes were on the bride and groom except for mine. I was still focused towards the heavens, watching the six birds circle the newly weds over and over again in joyful unison. Those six birds represented six very special family members who were watching over my younger brother on his wedding day. From the vantage point of the heavens, our loved ones cherished and cheered on the union of the newly weds, just as they had promised.

That day was the beginning of a life-long relationship with my spiritually winged friends. Anytime I was feeling down, needing support or just looking for some guidance, I started to notice there was always a bird there to set my mind at ease. I have had birds follow my car down the highway during my entire 10km trek into a dreaded day of work. The birds gracefully fly low and beside my vehicle as if to say, "have no fear, we will be by your side the entire journey." I have had birds land outside my window and peer in at just the right time to offer their support. I have had feathers left to me as gifts and inspiration when I needed it the most. And I have had birds perch next to me while I am out in my yard communing with nature. These winged creatures have been a blessing in my life, and I am so honored to hear their words of wisdom and feel the love they emanate. Birds have literally lifted me up and have guided me towards my SOULworks.

A few years after my first encounter with birds, I was attending a spiritual retreat and listening to a native elder talk about his spiritual encounters. It was at that time he referenced my connection with birds and called me the Bird Lady. He also encouraged me to believe in my abilities and myself, something I had certainly been struggling with my entire life. Hearing his words of wisdom made my confidence soar. I had received confirmation, yet again, that I was on the right path. With his short but very accurate observation, I became more comfortable and confident in who I was, and the gifts I had to share.

Activating your SOULworks

Angels, spirit guides, and our departed loved ones are always by our side, and are always willing and able to help out in times of need. Spirit guides truly want to be a part of our lives: enjoying our happiest moments, supporting us through the toughest of times, and helping to ensure our life experiences are memorable. The spirit world watches over us 24/7, providing round the clock inspiration and support. They cherish their opportunity to interact on a daily basis, and appreciate being recognized as an active part of our lives.

I am blessed to have established the presence of these divine beings and actively embraced their existence into my life at an early age.

However, even if you have never thought about your spirit guides before today, it is never too late to start. Your angelic team is as anxious to be a part of your life as you are in theirs. Their involvement is not a job interview we have to conquer or a test we have to pass. Their love is infinite and their reach unsurpassable. There is no question too small, support too trivial or magical moment too late, to involve the spirit world. So what are you waiting for?

Believing in the spirit world is the first step to making their interactions a reality. Even if you do not see, hear, feel, smell or know without a doubt they are there, you only need to trust and believe with an open mind. If I had approached the bird sitting on my hand as nothing more than a freak coincidence, my heart would never have opened to hear the blessed words from my loved ones. If I had been annoyed by the bird's wing sweeping across my cheek, I would never have looked towards the heavens for an answer. Without an open mind, this wonderful story of my departed loved ones actively watching and being a part of my brother's wedding, would have been lost forever. Start watching for the signs and synchronicities demonstrating the presence of your angelic team. The signs are there, you only need to open your mind and journey on the path within your heart to find them.

Watching for divine signs are a common practice and a wonderful way to witness the power of spirit. However, I do consider this method to be a passive interaction with the divine. My preference is to actively solicit their involvement. For example, instead of wishing my dear Grandma Annie would pay me a visit from the spirit world, I started to invite her for a visit every morning during teatime. Even though I could not physically see her presence, I did start having conversations and expecting to hear an answer. Over time, our mornings together began to blossom until it became a daily routine we both looked forward to. Sometimes, we just sit and enjoy each other's company. Other times, we talk about my future or reminisce about the past. There are also moments Grandma Annie provides a shoulder to cry on or the encouragement to move forward along my path. Anyone who knows the two of us will attest to the strong bond we had while my grandma was among the living. Those who are open to spirit have also recognized the strong bond we continue to nurture to this very day. My dear Grandma Annie continues to be my rock, and it all started the day I suggested she drop by for tea.

Sure, at first I thought I was making it up, but eventually I could hear her laugh, see her smile, and sense her loving energy. The key to the spirit world is through your imagination. This is not because you are making it up. It is because you are moving away from your logical mind that questions encounters with the other side. Once secure in the openness of your imagination, you energetically free yourself from the constraints of our world, and begin to reconnect with the divine.

Your Move:

- ❑ **Expect an answer.** Do you want to hear from a deceased loved one? Actively start the conversation and expect an answer. The response may be a flash image within your mind, the melody of a song, a bird flying by or a vivid response within your dreams. When it comes to communicating with spirit, the possibilities are endless, when we view the world with endless possibilities.

- ❑ **Establish a routine to convene with spirit.** Initially it helps to have a specific time or location in which to talk with your angelic team. Once the intention has been set and contact made, continue to verbalize to your spirit guides throughout the day. Honor them by utilizing their life coaching skills and lifetimes of wisdom. Your guides will reciprocate with answers to your everyday questions, and assist you with your deepest desires. Talk to them like they are one of your best friends and an active participant in your life, because they truly are.

❑ **Develop your symbolic language.** You can either make your own meanings for symbols or you can buy books to utilize. The important step is to hold the intention that for your purposes, "blank" will symbolize "blank". For example, there are many books I have collected over the years. I utilize these interpretation books when conversing with my spirit guides: a dream interpretation book, a number interpretation book, and an animal spirit guides book. There are many wonderful resources out there and they are all very beneficial. The key is to hold the intention that the symbolism contained within the pages of these books, will be the information utilized when communicated with spirit. Once this basis is established, your guides will utilize the books you have purchased for communication. I often have visions of objects, encounter numbers or experience flash images of animals, that I later reference within the books to discover the hidden message from my guides. I have also come to create a lot of my own symbolism. For example, I believe owls represent wisdom or a wise decision. Therefore, if I were to see an owl in response to a particular scenario I have asked my guides, I would consider my initial thoughts of proceeding down a specific path in question, a wise one.

❑ **Increase your vibration.** For those of us who still live and reside on the earth plane, our vibrational energy is far denser than the energy of the spirit world. Meet your spirit guides in the middle, by increasing your own energy field. This can be accomplished by spending time in nature, singing, eating healthy, maintaining a positive outlook on life, exercising, and even simply smiling more often. The higher your vibration, the stronger the connection to the spirit world. Take this one step further and hold the intention your vibration is increasing while conducting these activities. While exercising, imagine your body becoming filled with light. Watch as any thoughts, experiences or beliefs that are no longer serving you to your highest good are simply melting away and running off you along with your sweat. While eating, envision the food being filled with light and increased vibrational energy. Know that your food is a gift from Source and is to be enjoyed.

❑ **Develop patience and persistence.** This may sound like an oxymoron, but the two concepts work hand in hand. In terms of patience, acknowledge and understand the spirit world does not always rotate around our earthly schedules. Even though you may whole-heartedly want a miraculous intervention or message from spirit today, does not mean you will immediately receive one. There may be far greater life plans underway or lessons you have yet to understand. Learn to expect spirit's active involvement in your life, but honor their wisdom and divine timing. In terms of persistence, ensure your spiritual growth is a priority, and continue to expand your awareness. If one method of communication does not work, try another. Spiritual growth is an ongoing, lifelong, learning process. It takes time, dedication, and an unwavering heart.

CHAPTER 6

Early Memories of the Unexplained

L ooking back there were plenty of signs showing me a world that I could only dream was possible. There were magical and mystical moments that reconnected me to who I truly was, giving me a glimpse of my inner light and soul potential. However, I grew up in a family dynamic that did not discuss mystical experiences, and so I was left confused, scared, and vulnerable to the unknown. It was not until much later in life, that I could look back with awe and sheer appreciation of the messages and gifts that have shaped my entire life.

As a child, I grew up in a family that was religious. Not spiritual, just religious. I distinguish the two because I have always felt that religion provides an external means for those seeking to have someone else give them the answers to this world. To give them a textbook explanation on the way things surely are. Religion teaches society how to send a hopeful prayer, interpret the Bible, worship the Lord, and anxiously await a miracle.

Those that are spiritual on the other hand, believe in themselves and the power of their own inner wisdom. They not only know they are connected to the divine, there is a strong and continual two-way communication that is always taking place; an inner knowing that life is more than what we perceive within our limited earthly senses. A knowing that we are all connected and hold the power within ourselves to create miracles and live a life of peace, health, and happiness.

The kicker is, each soul must learn to see their inner light and let it shine. No one person, religion or organization can do the work for you. External resources can and should be used to help you sort through the clutter; however, you must be the driving force behind your own SOULworks. As I stand as a wonderful example of the ups and downs encountered during this process, I can clearly demonstrate how the path of spiritual growth is not always achieved with grace and ease, but achievable it most certainly is.

My first experience with the unknown occurred in grade three, when my young uncle died in a tragic accident. I remember the day very clearly. From my perspective, it was not a sad day at all, for I understood where he was going, and more importantly I understood that he was still in my life, just in a different way. I also distinctly remember understanding all of this at least two weeks before the accident actually happened.

The day a family member did eventually come to my grade school with the news of his passing, I was so very confused. "I have some sad news," my aunt began, "your uncle has died and is no longer with us." After hearing her words, mass confusion whirled around in my little mind, as I tried to comprehend the conversation. She must be lying! He most certainly was with us, and why was everyone so sad? Had we not accepted this truth and known he was ready to leave a few weeks ago?

This experience was truly a baffling one for me. It was the first death in my family that I could remember. Everyone told me I had to say goodbye, and that I would not see my uncle again until I was up in heaven. If that was true how come I could still feel his presence?

It is always difficult for people to understand the death of a loved one. To me, it is not a death. It is a homecoming that I have never feared. I see it as a graduation from this school here on earth. However, it was not until years later that I found books and people that agreed with my youthful perspective of life. A perspective that knows we are only here on earth to experience life, and that as tragic as they may seem, on a soul level we choose our exit points to return back home. If only I had been able to understand that reality as a young child, my life would have made so much more sense. Instead, I felt like an outsider: homesick and confused.

Looking back, there were many moments in life that conflicted with what had been explained to me as truths. Orbs of light used to swim merrily around my room at night. I distinctly remember asking my parents why they were there, only to be met with more confusion when told it was just my imagination. A room darkening blind and nightlight still could not stop these orbs from appearing in the night. But, they did stop me from asking any more questions about the subject. The lights never actually made me afraid; they were fun, calming, and gave me a happy feeling. They became my secret nightlife into the world beyond.

Please do not get me wrong. I do not blame my parents for not understanding. I know they were working within their own realities and experiences, that over time, had become clouded with societies perception of normal. However, it is that clouded perception that I feel the need to help society lift. The veil to the other world is thinning, and people need to understand they are not alone in these experiences. As an adult, I have now been able to identify these orbs of light as spiritual beings. Loved ones, spirit guides, and angels that provide me with comfort and support. What a wonderful reality.

Like any teenage girl, I also spent a significant amount of time looking at myself in the mirror. Not because of vanity, but because I was intrigued by my body. At one point, while staring into the mirror, my fifteen-year-old face began to slowly morph into that of an older lady. Startled, I quickly sat back and tried to regain my composure after seeing another version of myself staring back through the mirror. As I became more interested in this phenomenon, I used to spend hours looking into the mirror, watching my face change from a teenage girl, to an older lady, to a native elder, and then back again. Never did the faces feel like strangers; rather, I felt a connection to these people and felt that on some level I knew who they were. Checking in with my Google references at the time (friends, family, and the library), I never did find anyone who understood what I was describing. This void of knowledge once again left me feeling confused and frustrated. It also added another secret to my ever-growing vault of taboo subjects.

Years later, I found articles and testaments of others that have experienced similar occurrences, and the minute I heard their interpretation, I instantly felt at peace. Many believe that we have lived many lives on this earth. That our soul reincarnates time and time again to learn life lessons and to experience new and different things. It was then that I started to grasp the concept of just how many lives I have lived. I finally understood that my days in front of the mirror showed brief reflections and glimpses into my past.

The last monumental experience of my youth is what I refer to as my shut down point. Many of us have them. These are the times that we are faced with a situation that scares us into shutting down our sixth senses, and closing off from our spiritual self. For me, it happened in high school. I was in grade seven and at an all-night fundraiser for the school. I was awkwardly in the stage of trying to fit in, blending in with the crowd, and finding myself in the vast sea of adolescence; a terrifying life stage to begin with. Throw into the mix a lack of sleep, a noisy group of kids, and not enough food to keep me grounded, and you have a recipe for disaster. At some point near the end of the night, I started to hear things: peoples' thoughts, far-off voices I had never heard before, and just general chaos. My perception of time also started to speed up, and I started to feel like I was not even in my body anymore. The noise was confusing and it scared me. I ended the night of my "cool entry into high school" crying in the corner like a first grader. I had to be escorted out of the school, while stating that I thought I was going crazy and yelling at the voices to be quiet. Voices that only I seemed to be able to hear.

I never did understand at the time what had happened and would not fully comprehend this moment until years later. I clearly remember the experience, I remember asking the voices to stop, and unfortunately, I remember being humiliated in front of the whole school. And, unlike my other spiritual and psychic encounters as a child, this one I never spoke of to anyone. I never questioned what happened; I never sought out advice. I just shut down.

Part of my SOULworks is to ensure people understand they do not need to feel confused or alone. Spiritual events do happen in our lives that are outside of society's current perspectives. We are in constant contact with loved ones, angels, and the divine. We can utilize our sixth senses of sight (a.k.a. clairvoyance), sound (clairaudience), feeling (clairsentience), smell (clairalience), and knowing (claircognizance), to access information from the spiritual realms. We only need to open our hearts, minds, and souls to allow the experience in. It is time.

<u>Activating your SOULworks</u>

The world through the eyes of a child is an amazing one. This era of our lives is filled with miraculous moments and encounters with the divine our young minds cannot fully grasp within today's society. Yet as adults, we are often too close-minded to truly see the depths of our souls. Adults are quick to tell children how things "truly" are without realizing we are the ones who have lost touch with the truth.

During adolescence, our connection with spirit is strong and vibrant. The children of today are coming into this world with all of their sixth senses fully operational. Our children remember life on the other side, and if asked, can provide details on past lives and soul encounters. They often see energy, hear and communicate with the spirit world, and interact telepathically. However, when raised in a home where these gifts are not recognized or explained, their experiences quickly move to the background and are forgotten.

If you want to expand your awareness, view our world through the eyes of a child. Be open to new ideas and take a second look at past notions dismissed for centuries. Believe in magic and our ability to live as higher vibrational beings. Know that we are not alone.

Your Move:

- ❑ **Observe children.** We gain to learn so much from our children. These bright old souls are returning to earth to provide lifetimes of wisdom and insights. Silently observe the children in your life. Watch as a baby's eyes light up or their smiles widen at the spirits all around you. Notice the conversations children have with imaginary friends, and believe for even just a moment the experiences are real. Acknowledge past connections between children and adults;

know this is not the first lifetime you have had together. Notice how children are energetically drawn to nostalgic toys of their past childhoods when marketing and advertising do not interfere. Watch and learn.

❑ **Acknowledge experiences.** Review your own childhood and notice synchronicities that have shaped your life today. Do you remember having imaginary friends nobody else acknowledged? Were there moments of your youth where time seemed to speed up or stand still? What are some of the magical elements in life you used to believe in: fairies, elves or angels? Consider just for one moment these mythical creators do exist within our world, but just on a different vibrational frequency. Open your mind. In fact, step out and make an effort to connect with these magical beings. Sit outdoors and invite the fairies into your world. Give a tree a hug, and notice how the tree will energetically give you a hug back (seriously, try it). Stop mocking lawn ornaments and place an elf in your garden. To do so, is to acknowledge their presence and welcome them into your world.

❑ **Dabble with the unknown.** Ask your guides and angels to help increase your vibration and connect with the other side.

○ Try mirror gazing to catch a glimpse of your own soul.

○ Venture on a soul quest by fasting and meditating upon a candle.

○ Watch the open air and observe movements in the energetic space.

○ Enjoy sitting in silence so you can listen to your inner wisdom.

○ Try speaking to a tree or a rock. They have been on this earth a lot longer than you have, and hold lifetimes of wisdom. Elements of our earth are vibrational energy as well; they hold many secrets and reflections of our world. Ask them for guidance and trust the answers received.

○ Endeavor working with crystals. Notice what crystals you are drawn to and interpret their meaning. Crystals are a wonderful source of high vibrational energy. Once you have established a collection, pick one a day to carry with you. Not only will you be receiving the energy from the crystal, you will also receive guidance.

○ Buy yourself a pendulum or a deck of angel cards. All these tools are wonderful ways to gain insights and wisdom for your soul.

❑ **Talk openly.** Start communicating and expressing your experiences if only to yourself. I spent years hiding from my spiritual encounters because they scared me. Do not be afraid. Talk to the children in your life. Ensure they feel comfortable expressing their magical moments with the other side. Expand your awareness together.

CHAPTER 7

Manifesting Mastered

We live in a world where everyone has more and more possessions in their life. Ironically, we also live in a world where people feel they never have enough. People always want what they do not have. We are always searching for more, always looking for something better. I am no exception. I continually find myself always wanting to achieve and obtain more and more, regardless of how much I have accomplished in my life. Seems I am never content with what I currently have, and am driven to reach for more.

I used to think this perspective on life was unhealthy. Some parts of it are; like how society has continued to expand our material wealth with little to no consideration for the planet. Or how our personal possessions have literally become disposable, as we greedily shop to own the latest and greatest of everything.

There are, however, many good aspects to this soulful drive. As we crave more satisfaction out of life, we are striving to achieve all that we can be and learning how to manifest the life we truly desire. This is how to live a divinely inspired life. We are pushing ourselves to have the best possible experience in this lifetime and that is a good thing. The further we push ourselves, the more we tap into the universal wisdom and propel society forward. It is this forward movement that successfully implements change in the world. Change is evolution. It is what takes us out of our comfort zones and pushes us to be the best we can be.

One of the first times I learned to manifest started out to be, what I thought at the time, was a compromise. My husband and I were looking to relocate and were really interested in moving away from the hustle and bustle of city life. Owning an acreage was our true dream, and we started our search with excitement and anticipation. As we shopped around looking for the perfect place to call our home, we were becoming more and more restless at how hard it was to acquire one. Our options were very limited, and they all seemed to lack the qualities we were truly seeking. After considerable time looking over the real estate market, my husband finally suggested I make my top five list of must haves. It was becoming obvious to both of us we would never afford the kind of home we truly desired.

I started making my list, and quickly realized I actually only had five items on my wish list of priorities: ten acres of property, 15 minutes or less to the city, biking distance from a small town that did not require my children to cross the highway, located on a quiet road, and a few neighbors in the area so we were not in the middle of no-where. There it was, my entire wish list in five simple points. How hard could that be?

List or no list, many of the acreages we saw at the time were either too expensive or too far away from the city. Our excitement once again started to dwindle, and we resigned ourselves to the fact that acreage life for our family was perhaps not meant to be. Instead, we changed gears entirely and spent our days looking at houses within a few small towns near the city. We were hoping something would catch our eye, but nothing really did. Our hearts longed for acreage living.

On the way home after a long and frustrating day of house hunting, we drove past another real estate sign indicating there was an acreage for sale. We had followed many of these signs over the last few months and were really not up for the disappointment. Besides, it was getting late, we were very tired, and our patience was wearing thin. However, despite our thoughts to just throw in the towel, something pulled us down that gravel road. Maybe this would be the one, we reasoned. How long could it possibly take to have one quick look?

When we reached our destination, we were both so very disappointed yet again. This time, there was no house at all; only a flat piece of pasture land for sale. Frustrated by the day's events and our hopeless situation, we continued down the road heading for home. As luck would have it, the road was a dead-end and so we looped around and headed back out the way we had arrived. As we drove past the piece of property that was for sale, our van died. Right there, it just died. Wow, the universe must really be laughing at us right now, we thought. Talk about adding insult to injury.

My husband set out to walk for help, leaving the kids and me in the van to wait. As I sat there in all of my frustrations in this unfamiliar territory in what seemed like the middle of nowhere, I quietly asked my angels why this had to happen. Why could our day not have gone smoother and our dreams achieved? Their response was short but soothing, "Look where you are." I slowly looked around and became overwhelmed with gratitude at where our van had stopped. Miraculously, we were sitting right in front of the For Sale sign again. But it was not the sign that got me excited. It was the location. The property looked to be 15 minutes or less from the city, biking distance from a small town that did not require my children to cross the highway, the land was located on a quiet road, and a few houses were scattered in the neighborhood. Humbled, I quickly realized our van had not quit in the middle of nowhere. Our van had quit right in the location of our future home.

By the time my husband returned with help, I anxiously told him of my discovery. We contacted the realtor the very next morning and made an offer on the ten acres of property (did I forget to mention the property size ended up being ten acres too?). We did purchase the land, built our home, and achieved the goals we set out to accomplish. Looking back over the experience, I am so grateful the universe found a way to make us take a second look at what seemed like a hopeless situation. By providing us with that brief moment in time, we were able to pause, reflect, and accept the gift spirit was so clearly presenting to us, our dream home.

The next time you are in a situation that seems hopeless, I encourage you to take the time to pause and reflect. Is the situation really hopeless or are you hopelessly dismissing a gift from the divine? It is true; in my situation, we did not actually get a home with the initial purchase of the property. However, upon closer reflection when I went back to review the five items on my wish list, I quickly realized a house had never actually been included. Our dream home was all about location, location, location. My entire wish list had been manifested right before my eyes, and I am forever thankful I took the time to remember to open them.

Since that day, I work hard to manifest the things I want in my life. My dreams, goals, and visions of having a blessed life and being a world-renowned healer are becoming a reality and it feels great. Never feel bad for striving for greatness, for you are here to have the best experience possible. If we positively declare our dreams and wishes, the universe will help us to manifest an inspired life, and help to create a peaceful reality that is like heaven on earth. In fact, manifesting our world in a respectful and loving way, will be the catalyst that helps save our planet. Do not overlook this gift. Start actively making a difference in your world and the world all around you. It is time for change. We are co-creators of this universe and keeping yourself small does not serve you or anyone else.

Activating your SOULworks

The concept of co-creating our world comes second nature to a number of people, and to others it is completely misunderstood. Some people welcome this concept with open arms and others dismiss its validity entirely. However, even if you are unaware of your abilities to inspire your world or disbelieve in its merits, rest assured you have and always will be energetically creating your life and surroundings with your thought forms. Therefore, you might as well learn how to harness this universal energy.

I find those who are content with life, tend to agree with the concept of manifesting our world through our thoughts. Their wealth can be in many forms, but in all cases, those who are inspired to manifest, work hard for their achievements and are very proud of their accomplishments in life. On the other hand, I find those who lack the elements they desire, whether the focus is financial, material possessions or personal relations, do not agree with the concept of being responsible for creating their world. For some reason these people prefer to go with the attitude that life is hard, and they are hard done by. Countless amounts of their energies are put towards believing nothing ever goes their way, and everyone else always catches the lucky breaks in life. Which category do you fall into?

There is no harm in striving to create and achieve everything you want in your life. In fact, it is a much more practical use of your time and energy than focusing on what you do not have or wallowing in self-pity. If there are elements in your life you wish to change or enhance, then for heaven's sake put some energy and positive thought forms towards creating it. There is really no limit to what you can manifest in your world. As evolution and the advancement of society have shown, if you can dream it, you can achieve it. The key is to clearly set your intentions of what it is you would like to create, and then act upon opportunities that come your way.

Your Move:

- ❑ **Start small.** I have learned to manifest anything I truly desire. You can too. All you really need to do is state your intentions, ask your guides and angels for support, and then trust it is being taken care of. No desire is too small or want too large. Everything you yearn for can be created and manifested. Is the grass always greener on the other side? If so, make a conscious effort to bring more green into your world. Start familiarizing yourself with this universal force by making simple requests to expand your repertoire. Silently request a visit from a friend this week, then sit back and watch who enters your life. State your intentions to find a specific item while out shopping, then follow your inner guidance to the perfect sale. Put some positive thought forms towards some quiet time by yourself, then notice as everything around you starts falling into place.

- ❑ **Give thanks.** When everything in your life begins to fall into place, do not dismiss this as just coincidence. Give thanks where thanks are due. You are responsible for helping to create your inspired life, and your guides are also helping to ensure your wants and needs are met. Reflect back to past successes in your life and notice the key elements that made your goals possible. Start to notice the synchronicities all around you. Write down the requests you have made and then accept the results with open arms. Do not dismiss what comes into your life because it was not exactly as you had imagined. Perhaps it will turn out even better.

❑ **Develop your wish list.** Carefully review all areas of your life and determine the components you would like to enhance. This could be anything, so dream big. Would you like to manifest a more satisfying career, additional free time, a new home, the perfect mate, financial freedom, spiritual enlightenment? The possibilities are endless. Brainstorm each area of interest further and add in the details. Similar to my top five priorities for a home, start putting thought into what it is you truly want. Be honest with yourself and include all your deepest desires. Do not leave things off your list just because you think it will never be possible. In fact, do yourself a favor and leave this attitude behind. To manifest an inspired life, you must remain confident and trust in the outcome.

I also always like to add to my list of manifestations the magical phrase, "I wish to achieve at minimum these results or better. Thanks be to God." Be as specific as possible without narrowing your focus too much. Create a final copy of the list and start to visualize your success.

❑ **Summon your angelic team.** I cannot say this enough: your spiritual guides are here to help create an inspired life. Always remember to involve your divine team in all that you do, including manifesting your life's desires. Ask for their involvement, trust in your triumph, and then release your wishes towards the heavens. Continue to send positive energy towards your goal.

❑ **Take action.** You are able to manifest your world, but you also need to make an effort to follow your intuition.

Once you have put your true wishes and desires out into the world, watch for the opportunities that follow and do not be afraid to take action. So, if you put a thought form out into the universe to meet someone special and a few days later a friend suggests a double date, please do yourself a favor and say yes. The world can work in miraculous ways and opportunities will in fact knock on your door. However, you do have to recognize when an opportunity presents itself. If you are waiting for your special someone to be delivered straight to your door with a sign on their forehead saying "I'm the one," you may be waiting a long time.

Opportunity presents itself through divine guidance and nudges. Step by step, your messages will guide you to the outcome. Manifesting your world is like playing a game of chess. Pay attention to your surroundings, check in with your intuition, and then make your next move.

CHAPTER 8

The Power of Love

S hortly after I started my SOULworks business, I was invited to join an energy circle. This was a group of like-minded people who joined together on a regular basis to channel energy towards each other. Kind of like a spiritual spa day.

Going into the group, I was very intimidated and my confidence level was rock bottom. These people were a collection of Reiki Masters and energy channelling professionals who had been working in the field for quite some time. I felt like a fish out of water, and was so nervous I could hardly relax. I was also the only new person to join the group. To say I felt a little anxious would be a huge understatement.

During the spiritual spa day, one of the participants had the opportunity to sit and relax, while the rest of us channelled energy towards them. Then we would rotate positions and someone else would have the chance to be the receiver. When we all started working on the first person, I felt like I could not even function. Usually, by this point in my life, I could literally feel the energy coming out of my hands when working on someone. That day nothing was flowing. It was like my well had run dry, and I was only sitting in the circle as an observer. My nerves were definitely interfering. I felt so inferior in this group and was having trouble calming myself down.

It was at that point I asked my guides and angels for assistance. The response was very clear, "just look at your client with sincerity and the process will begin." My eyes had been closed already, so I opened them back up and sat there looking at this lady in front of me. In her, I saw myself: someone who just wanted to belong; someone who wanted to feel loved and be one with the universe; and more importantly, someone who was entrusting me to help her get there. With that, my heart opened straight up to this stranger sitting in front of me, and the energy started to flow. In fact, it flowed stronger than I had ever experienced before. The energy that day was so powerful to me, that it brought tears to my eyes. I closed those teary eyes, began to relax, and truly started to enjoy the moment.

My moment did not last very long, as I was jolted back out of my inner harmony by the sound of a voice. The lady receiving the energy was speaking. "Hey, you. What is your name again?" she asked in what I felt at the time was a very loud and intimidating voice. With my eyes still closed, my confidence began to dwindle. I found myself hoping by some grace of God she was talking to someone else. Of course, I knew better. I was the only one in the circle to whom she was not familiar.

Reluctantly I slowly started to open my eyes, sheepishly made eye contact and said in a very small, insecure voice, "my name is Lauren." She followed my prompting with a comment that made my heart sink. She indicated she was not sure what I was even doing and had never felt that way before. I quickly apologized and pulled my hands away feeling like all of my worst fears had just come true. Who was I to think I could do such important work and help channel energy from the heavens?

Then she spoke again. Her words sent energy racing down my spine and I will never forget her response. "Do not be sorry Lauren. I am saying it feels amazing. I can tell you are helping me shift and release blockages I have been working to change for years. What are you doing? Is that Reiki you are channelling? What did you say your modality was?"

I was speechless. I had just received the greatest gift any healer can ever receive: confirmation that I was on the right path and making a difference. But how would I gracefully answer her question? All eyes were focused my way expecting a response, and I had absolutely no idea what to say. No, it was not Reiki. I had never really taken any courses of any kind for energy healing. What was I going to tell them? To me it was instinct. It flowed naturally. Energy healing, I thought to myself, was LOVE. I kept my thoughts to myself though, and just humbly said thank you.

I will always be thankful for my experiences with this energy circle. They taught me to trust in my abilities and myself. This small group of like-minded people helped me gain the confidence I needed to go out in the world and truly start making a difference.

Years later, I am still often asked to explain what type of modality I use during my energy healing sessions. It is a fair question. I would ask the same. Thing is, it is still very difficult to explain what has grown to be years of life experiences, guidance, and intuition. How do you describe to someone how you breathe? Energy Healing is the same. It has become a part of who I am.

So why are there so many energy healing modalities out there, and which one is better than the next? They are all good. They all teach you how to look at the universe differently, how to channel energy, and how to help facilitate a positive change. Over the years, I have studied many forms of energy healing. As more and more people become interested in this field, more and more varieties will also become available. That is because we all add our own individual flare and our own unique approach to the healing wisdom of the ages.

However, regardless of how many different versions are created, they must all have two things in common. A successful healer must first BELIEVE in the power within herself/himself and the universe to create a positive energy shift in the body. And more importantly, she/he must channel that energy with LOVE. Pure, unconditional, straight from the heart, love. This dynamic duo is the classic healing modality that continues to stand the test of time. Regardless of what other names it may be given along the way, a strong belief system and a whole lot of love is what true miracles are made of. That is my modality. That is my SOULworks.

Activating your SOULworks

We are all healers. We all have the ability to channel healing energy and direct the light of Source energy towards someone or something in need. It is an innate gift from the divine and one of the most misunderstood abilities of our time. A limited number of people are clearly very gifted in the field of energy healing, and have instinctively utilized this powerful source to manifest change in the world around them. Others have sought knowledge in the field and have learned to utilize these skills to help facilitate positive changes of the body, mind or soul. Similar to how various individuals are born athletes, musicians or leaders; there are those among us who are naturally talented in the area of healing. However, that is not to say that we do not all possess the ability to learn. I may not be able to naturally compose a musical masterpiece, but if I have the passion or determination to expand my musical abilities, I am most certainly able to learn. Likewise, anyone who is passionate and determined to successfully work with energy healing, can and will in fact do so.

I truly believe evolved souls such as Yeshua and Buddha are examples of the potential that resides within all people. These expanded souls were able to achieve enlightenment while here on earth. Their knowledge in the field of healing came naturally and their purpose was to demonstrate to mankind the power we all have within us. Unfortunately, these lessons have been misunderstood and misrepresented for centuries. Our society has neglected to learn from their example. It is in finding this innate ability and connection with the divine, that our society will shift consciousness and advance the human race.

Your Move:

❑ **Send loving thoughts**. The next time you or someone in your life is in need, help by sending love and inspirational thoughts. Do not send worry, fear or judgment. In terms of energy, negative thought forms, words, and actions only add fuel to the fire. Instead, utilize kind and gentle thoughts and keep your intentions positive. Use your imagination to direct glorious light and surround the situation with heavenly thoughts. Create in your mind the perfect scenario, and trust in your ability to help make it so.

❑ **Believe in yourself.** Nobody can accomplish this task for you. I can believe in you. God can believe in you. But only you can truly believe in yourself and your ability to heal. I urge you to understand you are worthy and capable. You are all able to tap into the divine energy source of spirit and utilize this gift to positively co-create your world. So, what are you waiting for? Give it a try. Send positive thoughts to an upcoming situation you feel is hopeless. Ask your angels and guides for assistance on creating a more positive outcome.

Believe in your power to make a difference. Change the outcome.

❑ **Step up and make a difference.** Change never happens when you continue to stay within your comfort zone. To evolve as a healer, believe in your abilities and strive to make a difference.

○ Visit a hospital and silently send healing energies to those in need. Trust you have made a difference and observe as those who have suffered slowly begin to change their demeanor.

○ Scan the current news stories and instead of getting caught up in the gory details, send light and love out into the world. Watch as the outcome becomes more positive in the days to follow. Never doubt for one minute you were a contributing factor.

○ Approach those you have judged in the past with a new set of eyes. Honor them by accepting who they are and the difficult path they have chosen. Help them along their journey by surrounding them in light and trusting they are on their chosen path of life experiences. Go even further and shower them with random acts of kindness.

○ Proactively utilize positive thoughts and deeds, striving to become a role model for those around you. Without judgment or ridicule, send love from your heart to those who are continuously negative. Monitor their changes in attitude and luck.

○ Understand that all healings are successful at some level whether it is the body, mind or soul. Sometimes the process takes time and the order is not necessarily clear. Often you have to heal emotional issues before a physical healing will occur. However, trust the energy will go wherever it is needed.

❑ **Review all of your thought patterns.** Take an inventory of all your beliefs. Review the biblical scriptures with new eyes. Learn from those who have gone before you. You are able to become an active participant in your future and ensure it is a positive one. Release any old thoughts, experiences or beliefs that are no longer serving you to your highest good. Change the way you view your world. Approach life with a loving heart and a positive mind. Expect miracles.

CHAPTER 9

Amazing Grace

Somewhere along the way, the song Amazing Grace has become the melody of my soul. The lyrics uplift me, connect me to spirit, and bring me peace. The song speaks of surrendering to grace (spirit). It is about finding your way along the path of enlightenment, standing in your own true power with unwavering faith.

The first time I truly connected to this song was during a rough patch in my spiritual life. It was early on in my mystical endeavors and I was looking for answers. I knew I was connecting with spirit, but was still struggling to understand my abilities. My confusions and frustrations were at an all time high on the day I finally thought to ask my guides for support. I spoke up and pleaded, saying I knew they were in fact there and to please help guide me down the right path. I admitted to the confusions I felt when my spiritual experiences were different than the teachings of my upbringing. I asked why I saw the world differently than so many others around me. I asked for a more traditional or religious reference to help bridge the gap between the two points of view; something to validate my experiences. Then the words just started to flow....*Amazing Grace, how sweet the sound, that saved a wretch like me. I once was lost but now am found, was blind, but now I see....*

The song Amazing Grace was dearly loved by my grandparents, sang in church for generations, and is well known throughout the world, and yet I had not thought of it in years. Gently sung by a choir of angels, the lyrics were used to confirm my experiences and validate my connection to the spirit world. I was no longer blind to the light and grace within myself. I was clearly seeing the connection we all have with the divine. The song continued...

T'was Grace that taught my heart to fear; And Grace, my fears relieved. How precious did that Grace appear the hour I first believed...

The song is also about letting go of fears and trusting in the protective hands of the almighty. So not only was I being asked to see the potential within myself, I was being asked to let go of my fears and move forward with my gifts.

Through many dangers, toils, and snares I have already come. 'Tis Grace that brought me safe thus far and Grace will lead me home.

The last chorus I heard that day reminded me how far I had come. How much I had already accomplished in life, lessons I had learned, and hurdles I had climbed. And yes, grace would continue to lead me down the right path. I had asked for validation of my gifts and confirmation to move forward, and I certainly received the answers to my prayers. I just never expected them to be sung.

That was my first experience with the song Amazing Grace, but it would certainly not be the last. Whenever I am having an off day, I hear the choir of angels healing my emotional wounds with their angelic song. Oftentimes, I will even sing along. My voice is not angelic, but they do not seem to mind. I like to sing in harmony with the angels and let our souls blend through the beat of the music.

I am not the first one to discover the benefits of music to the body, mind, and soul. Music has always held inspirational status for many. It has been used since the beginning of time and echoes the reflection of the soul. Sound therapy is also becoming more prevalent as society moves towards embracing alternative health options. I myself, utilize sound vibrations for my personal development, and also to help increase the strength and intentions of my energy healing sessions.

Singing is one of the best ways I have found to connect and open the door to spirit, and Amazing Grace is my magical key. At one point, while studying healing at a spiritual college abroad, this song would also prove beneficial to others. It was during an experimental evening and we were trying to contact spirits during a good old-fashioned table tipping. For those unfamiliar with this term, it is when a group of people gathers for the purpose of contacting spirit and receiving communication via a table. The table is kind of like a very large pendulum or Ouija board. The participants ask spirit questions and spirit answers by moving the table.

The table we used was tall and skinny, more like a stool really; however, it was certainly big enough to ensure I was skeptical over the entire undertaking. Yes, I had played with pendulums and other spirit communication tools in the past with great success, but a table was certainly a new experience. My ego even reminded me of hoaxes I had heard, involving spirit seekers who would use tricks to move tables and claim the presence of spirits. Despite my skepticism, I was determined to enter the evening with an open mind. The group started by forming a circle around the table. The plan was to inspire a spirit to move the table, establish what a 'yes' and 'no' response looked like, and then start asking the spirit questions.

The group was all very excited and we started the evening with great anticipation. Our circle was formed and we started the process by raising the vibration of the room in an effort to make it easier for spirit to connect. Originally, this was done through listening to music as we all swayed back and forth in our chairs, staring at the table with excitement. Fifteen minutes passed and still no movement. Perhaps spirit did not like our choice of music. Another song selection was decided upon, and once again the room sat eagerly on standby waiting for our first visit from the spirit world. Once again, there was no movement in the table.

The group moved on and began to formulate Plan B. Plan B was to send energy to the table; after all, we were a group of healers. Everyone began to concentrate and send the table as much energy as we could muster. Time moved. The table did not.

All the while this was going on, I was having a silent conversation with my deceased Grandma Annie. I teased her to come through and move the table for the group. Her response was simple, "sing Amazing Grace the way you do when you think no one is listening, and I will move the table for you."

On to Plan C, the group would sing. I had not mentioned my conversation with grandma, but the idea to sing had surfaced amongst the group anyway. Don't you just love synchronicities? We all agreed this was a wonderful idea. Singing was very inspirational and would surely raise the vibration of the room. For another fifteen minutes the group sang many familiar tunes. Unfortunately, most of our selections were nursery rhymes. This was to ensure the large group of participants representing countries from all over the world would know the lyrics. I must admit, '*Twinkle Twinkle Little Star*' and other childhood tunes did absolutely nothing to lift my spirits and ensure my energy was flowing, let alone the energy of spirit.

By now over 45 minutes had passed and the group was losing all hope. Again, I heard Grandma Annie coaxing me to sing Amazing Grace. I certainly did trust grandma would follow through and move the table if I sang, but unfortunately, I am kind of shy in front of groups and my singing is definitely a weakness. The only thing I could muster was to ask the man standing next to me to sing Amazing Grace. If he started, I promised to follow along. He agreed and we vowed to get the song going at our next opportunity. It took another few songs to pass before we had our chance. However, when we did finally sing Amazing Grace, it only took the very first line of the song to start the table rocking back and forth. In fact, the table made its way clear across the circle and stopped right in front of me. I kid you not. The table actually moved and made a beeline straight for me. Its movements mimicked someone shuffling the table from side to side, as it inched its way across the room right to me. Yes, even in the spirit world I can still depend on my wonderful Grandma Annie.

The group was elated and found it very difficult to contain our excitement. We quickly established the "yes" and "no" movements of the table. "Yes" was shown as a forward and backward swaying motion and "no" was side to side. Both motions were very easy to identify, and ironically represented someone nodding or shaking their head. Incredible! Once this was established I started to ask my grandma questions and she was very quick to respond. The entire room sat speechless as we watched in awe, the table rocked from side to side in immediate response to my inquiries.

Once my turn was complete, we sang again in order to conjure up another spirit. The table would then move around the circle to the next lucky participant whose family member was coming through from the spirit world. More questions were asked and more responses were received, as the table continued to rock the room. We continued on in this manner for over two hours, as different spirits were welcomed into the circle and given the opportunity to speak to a loved one. It was such an incredible experience. My grandma and I secretly giggled all night over how we sang the table to life.

Ironically the group tried many other songs throughout the evening to keep the vibration up and the table responding. Amazingly, Amazing Grace was the only song able to keep the energy flowing and spirit communicating. We must have sung Amazing Grace fifty times that night, making the group incredibly tired of the music selection by the end of the evening. Everyone except Grandma Annie and me, of course, who were still merely humming together to our favorite tune. It truly was an Amazing Grace.

<u>Activating your SOULworks</u>

There are many ways to connect to the spirit world, but song is certainly one of the most effective. Songs lift our spirit, open our heart, and effectively increase our vibration to connect with the spirit world. Thanks to my Grandma Annie, I have witnessed the ability of song to even move a table and connect with spirit. I have no doubt with enough hearts and positive intentions, song is powerful enough to bring heaven onto earth. But let's begin by just creating a stir within your soul.

There are a multitude of inspirational songs available and a plethora of new ones being created every day. Magical collections of sound have blessed our souls since the beginning of time. It is easy to identify an inspirational song capable of elevating your connection to spirit. The lyrics will be thought provoking and the musical interludes breathtaking. Just listening to the sound vibrations of a song will stir your inner light and leave you pondering the sheer awe and magnitude of its beauty.

We all have differing tastes of inspired music and that is a good thing. Our unique personal preference truly makes our world beautiful. There are many types of music out there and all contain inspiration and glory within the notes. Personally, I am primarily a country music fan, and have quite honestly always stayed away from traditional hymns. That being said, Amazing Grace is definitely my power song. The lyrics were angelically delivered at the absolute most perfect time in my life as a reminder of our grace within. Without an open mind, I would have quickly dismissed this magical key that has expanded my connection with spirit.

Your Move:

- ❑ **Find your power song.** Let your heart find the beat of your soul. Listen to a wide array of music and determine what selections truly make your heart sing and bring you closer to God. Always keep an open mind and ear to discover your signature song. In finding your unique soul groove, you will amplify your relationship with the divine. Continue to use your power song any time you want to shift your energy, lift your spirit or start a conversation with your angelic team.

- ❑ **Ask spirit to communicate through song.** Are you pondering the direction of your life or seeking guidance from above? You do not have to focus on your power song to receive an answer from the spirit world. Simply look to your spirit guides while randomly listening to music. When a song selection truly speaks to your heart, you will know you have found your answer. Take the time to review the lyrics and discover the hidden messages within.

- ❑ **Play with music.** You do not have to be the next Beethoven or Jimmy Hendricks to reap the benefits of creating your own music. There are many simple instruments available that can be used to commune with spirit and optimize your health. I myself, utilize a bison skin drum similar to what our native ancestors utilized. Drums, rattles, singing bowls or a classic tambourine are simple tools that have been used since the beginning of time to heal the sick or help attain an altered state. It is within these altered states, when our ego has moved to the side, that we are able to communicate with spirit. Get creative with music. Playing an instrument is a tribute to the heavens and a very effective way of raising your vibration.

❏ **Listen.** Spirit will speak to you in all sorts of ways. If you have a song constantly playing through your mind, take a closer look at the lyrics. Perhaps your higher self is trying to get a message across. If you coincidentally overhear a special song on the radio at just the right moment, never doubt for one minute your spirit guides are demonstrating their presence in your life. If there is a specific bird continually singing outside your window in the wee hours of the morning, instead of getting frustrated by the encounter, take a moment to consider the meaning behind the melody.

❏ **Sing with all your heart and soul.** If you are confident enough to progress from listening to actually singing an inspired song, the results will be pure bliss as you ultimately convene with the divine. Take this experience one step further, and bravely sing from your heart in harmony with a group of people within a chapel or acoustically pleasing space. The energy will be electrifying as the beat surges and pulses through your very being. The experience will undoubtedly confirm that a blessed interaction with the spirit world has taken place. Once the music stops, continue to listen with your inner ear. The choir of angels will be audible as they gracefully continue to harmonize, sending love and joy through the power of song.

CHAPTER 10

Dream Time

I am a dream walker. A dream walker is someone who utilizes their dream state to journey, heal, teach, learn, and ultimately work on a soul level while his or her body is peacefully resting in bed. I would describe dream walking as multi-tasking super-sized. Although I believe I have done this my entire life, it was not until more recently that I realized how productive I actually am during my sleep time. At one point, I believed I only experienced crazy and bizarre dreams because of an overactive imagination. I would visit strange lands, witness historical events or have premonitions on what is yet to come, without truly realizing what I was encountering was real. Even when the events would later transpire, I would always chalk them up to coincidence.

Looking back, I can clearly see how friends and family were always interested in hearing my dream stories. They were way more open to the dreams being something more than just fantasy or nightmares. I, however, was more skeptical. Yes, I did find my dreams odd at times and sometimes did wonder about their origin, but there was always an element of self-doubt. After all, just like you, I came into this world with no user manual to clearly explain all of these oddities within life. And so, I was always trying to logically clarify how I could have known future events before they occurred. Perhaps I had unconsciously heard about the situation the day before, I would reason. Even without realizing, I could have then conveniently added the scenario into my dreams. Yes, perhaps that was it.

After my first theory proved wrong time and time again, I was still always looking for plausible explanations. Maybe I was causing the events to happen. Was it possible to put enough energy behind an idea while sleeping to make it occur? Is it possible to accidentally create an event without even realizing it? Wow, that was a scary thought. Some of my dreams were about destruction, natural disasters, and human violence; surely my mind was not creating this chaos. Besides, my mind was usually full of more pleasant thoughts, I reasoned with myself. But if I was not causing it, where was the information coming from?

It took two large and distinctive dreams transpiring into actual events before I could finally bring clarity to my questions. Both events appeared in the news shortly after my dreams occurred, with me always knowing more details than the media. The facts were starring me straight in the face. Somehow, I was accessing details of the events as they transpired. Even though it would take many more experiences before I fully understood the scope of my dream walking, I could no longer deny I was in fact somehow walking the earth in spirit to access information at night.

The first event was unfortunately a missing persons case. I clearly witnessed in my dreams how events transpired the night an innocent young woman went missing. In my dream, I could see what she saw, feel how she felt, and even hear conversations as the night unfolded. I saw what the young lady was wearing, the car she was in, who was with her, where her body would be found, and specific events leading up to her death. On that note, I woke up with a start, my heart pounding.

It took a long time to calm myself down. After all, I had never really experienced anything so real, and it definitely shook me up. It was just a dream, I reasoned with myself. Everything is okay and I am safely at home in bed. Unfortunately, that was not the case for the actual young lady in my dreams. A few days later I scanned the news and saw a headline of a young woman who was missing. Murder was not yet suspected, but it was the description of her clothes and the car she was last seen in, that sent chills down my spine and made my heart sink.

Because I was so new at profiling a missing persons case, it took quite a while to get all of the facts straight. I found I originally misinterpreted some of the dream's symbolism, and so the first set of information I provided to the police was not enough to help find the body of the missing young lady. However, I knew without a doubt I had seen some of the details needed to help solve the crime and so I forged ahead. It took three separate dreams that were months apart to finally help put all the pieces of the puzzle together. I made many mistakes along the way and definitely did not provide all accurate details. So, although I would like to take credit for helping to find the body, it was not really my persistence that finally lead to the scene of the crime, it was the victim's determination and the diligence of the local police force.

This young lady had continued to show up in my dreams and entrusted me to forward further details on to the police. She provided insights to help clear up misconceptions and provided additional clues to help with the case. Her determination was commendable. Her family needed closure and she was determined to ensure they received it. Finding her body would not bring back their daughter, but it would help to heal some of their wounds and bring them peace. On the day her body was found, I woke up to find the spirit of this young lady standing in my room holding a bouquet of yellow roses. I immediately knew she was finally at peace. She thanked me that morning for never giving up on her; I, in turn, thanked her for believing in me. In truth, we were both yearning to be found. For her, it was her physical body enabling both herself and her family to move forward on their journey. For me, it was the discovery and validation of dream walking; an awareness needed to help propel my journey forward, the journey of my own SOULworks.

This event was followed by many trips to the bookstore, more information gathering, and more time spent trying to understand dreamtime. I was looking for answers on questions I had yet to even articulate. I knew this event was a big shift in my awareness and I sought to understand more.

The second major dream bringing clarity to my questions was a natural disaster. One night I had a very vivid dream of a tornado sweeping though our cabin area. At one point during the dream, I started to have the distinct feeling my dream was once again providing visions of reality. Instead of worrying, I stood firm and protected our cabin, as well as my son who was up at a summer camp in the area. I envisioned protective walls being placed around our cabin and the entire perimeter of the camp, and held the intention that all would be safe.

In the morning when it was confirmed a large plow wind had in fact gone through the area in the night, my husband and I took the day off work to go survey the damage, and to make sure everything was okay. The summer camp had been missed entirely by the storm by one mile, and all the children were safe. However, the area where our cabin was located was hit very hard with 100 foot trees uprooted everywhere, with cabins and trailers extensively damaged. Upon closer inspection, every single one of our neighboring cabins and yards were affected; except our cabin, which literally looked like invisible walls were protecting it from the destruction.

What an amazing and humbling discovery. Sure, it sounds crazy, but I have come to realize we do have the power to protect and heal people, places, and things at any time, even in our sleep. I actually believe I conducted healings for people and events during my sleep long before I even started to recognize and practice energy healing during the day. It just took me a long time to recognize the patterns.

Now, lets take this discovery a step further. Yes, I was remote-viewing both situations during my sleep, and yes, I did provide help. However, could I have done more? For the victim, sure, it was nice to help bring closure to the case, but could I have done anything to prevent the situation from happening in the first place? After all, I was provided details on how the entire night transpired. If I had realized the magnitude of the situation, could I have intervened sooner? And in the case of the tornado, I may have helped protect our family cabin and the summer camp, but what about all the other areas of destruction? Could I have changed my intention to completely snuff out the tornado all together? Is there a way to channel healing energies to people, places or things who are in need and ultimately help change the course of history?

I believe there is. On a smaller scale, I have already learned to recognize when energy is out of balance and have already learned how to help send light and healing energy to any situation. And, I am not the only one. There are many of us in the world who are discovering the same realities. To broaden our reach and make a larger impact on our world, we only need to widen our intentions and radiate even greater thought forms of love and light. I need to say this again, because I believe it will help change the course of our history. It is possible to recognize when energy is out of balance and learn to send light and healing energy to any situation. To broaden our reach and make a larger impact on our world, we only need to widen our intentions and radiate even greater thought forms of love and light.

Our world may appear to be in chaos and there are so many people out there just waiting for someone special to be born into this world to save us, to remove the darkness, save the planet, heal the sick, feed the hungry, and bring us peace. To this passive perspective on life, I echo what so many wise ones before me have indicated, "WE ARE THE ONES WE HAVE BEEN WAITING FOR."

The next step is to recognize, understand, and believe that we are the ones who will help bring joy and peace into our world once again. Please observe the current state of the world, but instead of wallowing in its impending destruction, breathe more light and love into it. Manifest the world we want to live in. Fight the darkness, fear, and hatred we humans have created by sending our world light, love, and hope into every situation and to every nook and cranny. We always had and always will have access to this light, this divine spark within us. Now please use it.

Activating your SOULworks

I believe dreaming occurs in direct correlation to the stages of our enlightenment. The more aware we become of our connection to spirit, the larger our dream experiences become.

Dreams are the gateway to the soul. They offer a glimpse into our most inner thoughts, fears, life purpose, and divine connection. It is a place to receive messages for our higher self. Dreams also offer a portal through which to connect to our guides and loved ones. This sacred dwelling represents a bird's eye view of our life and our progress along our soul path.

Dreams also help to heal our physical and emotional issues. It is during this peaceful state that our bodies rejuvenate and our minds expand. Our sleep time is like a large coffee break within our life's work. It is a coveted time to kick back, relax, and reconnect to the divine spirit within. Dreams allow our souls the freedom to guide our actions and encounters from above. Everyone dreams and is given this sacred space to convene with spirit and your higher self, even those who do not remember.

Lucid Dreaming occurs when we enter a state of awareness within our dreams and realize we are sleeping. During a lucid dream, we are able to become active participants within the dream and make a conscious effort to change the outcome. Where dreams allow our souls the freedom to guide our actions and encounters from above, lucid dreams allow our human counterpart to also become involved. Lucid dreaming is a raised consciousness while here on earth. It provides a glimpse of our abilities as a divine spirit to alter our outcomes in life. In this respect, lucid dreaming is a demonstration of our greatness and God-given potential within.

To *Dream Walk* is to expand our consciousness beyond our own soul, to look beyond our own individual path, and actively observe the paths of others. At this point, we are still connecting to our divine spirit; however, we are also moving into a space where it is possible to view the life works of others. The dreams and visions I encountered of the missing person's case is an example of dream walking. In my initial dream, I was remotely viewing the event as it was actually happening.

To *Lucid Dream Walk* is to further expand our consciousness to not only observe the paths of other people and situations, but to actively send light and love towards the scenario and help facilitate a more positive result. My tornado vision and protective action within a dream state is an example of lucid dream walking. I was remotely viewing and acting upon the destructive weather.

One more topic I would like to discuss is *Daydreaming.* We have the ability to accomplish the same benefits during a brief moment of reflection within a daydream, as we can in our sleep. We are still able to connect with our divine self and send positive intentions into our lives. Daydreaming is the canvas on which to create our future and our life is the masterpiece. Use moments throughout the day to masterfully dream your heart's desires.

Your Move:

❑ **Honor your sleep time.** The majority of society is sleep deprived. Ensure your body receives plenty of rest and down time. Recognize the benefits this peaceful opportunity provides to your body, mind, and soul on a daily basis. Take the time to relax and open your awareness. Provide yourself with the gift of a sacred routine before and after waking. Pay close attention to the images or insights you receive while going to sleep or just upon waking. This too can be a message from above. Give thanks for the opportunity to interact with the spirit world and rejuvenate your human self. Let go of any guilt for taking time to rest and simply enjoy.

❑ **Monitor your dreamtime.** Make a formal request to your higher self and your angelic team to utilize your dream space for guidance and insights. Even if you do not understand or remember your dreams, give thanks and acknowledge the communication opportunities offered within your sleep. Utilize a dream journal or recording device to keep track of your dreams. Use your own intuition to interpret their meaning and trust in your wisdom. If you find this difficult, refer to any dream interpretation book to delve further into the unknown. When recalling dreams, consider if the content is addressing unresolved past issues, present circumstances or future events. If there is a dream that continues to surface in your life, take a closer look to determine the messages within. Once you acknowledge the message, the recurring dream will often fade away.

❑ **Establish healing intentions.** Within the portal of our dream state, our bodies have the ability to heal. Sleep is a wonderful and much needed component to help overcome any illness or ailment. Trust your body is rebooting and your health is being restored. Actively set your intentions to send and receive any healing required for your highest good. Dreamtime can also be used to heal events, situations or outcomes. Even if you have not experienced lucid dreaming, you can still set your intentions prior to going to sleep to send healing energies towards a person, place or thing. Setting your intentions will summon your higher self to oversee the job, and ensure positive vibrations are being created. Once again, request assistance and support from your angelic team.

❑ **Believe big.** Dreaming opens your awareness and creates your realities. You do have the ability to heal and facilitate positive changes in your life during your dreamtime. Believe in this ability. A wise friend once told me "you can think big, but to truly create a big shift in life, you need to BELIEVE BIG". Believe in your God-given abilities to positively impact your life and the lives of those around you. While falling asleep, do not let your mind run over past events over and over again, like a broken record focusing on what could have been. Instead, focus on creating what will be. Allow yourself to just dream.

CHAPTER 11

Short but Sweet

I am very fortunate to have a very large collection of inspirational stories and experiences throughout my lifetime. Many of them demonstrate angelic intervention, miraculous healings, and spiritual encounters. However, I did want to take the time to point out not all spiritual moments are on such a grand scale. Of course, any time spent with spirit is grand, but the events do not necessarily need to be so extraordinary. In fact, many of the smaller encounters I have had with spirit are also some of the most memorable I hold dearest to my heart. They are the small whispers you hear when you wake up in the morning. The knowing you get when you look up at just the right moment to watch a butterfly gracefully approach with a message of hope from above. Or the conversations you overhear from passersby holding insights and wisdom on a topic you were just pondering.

I always watch for signs and use my intuition to direct my journey of life with grace and ease. Here are some of my personal favorite moments demonstrating spirit working around the clock to provide guidance and support. I encourage you to start watching for your short but sweet moments with the divine.

I shop at a thrift store for most of my family's clothes and household items. I just love a bargain and am also conscious of re-using items whenever possible to help preserve Mother Earth. If you think your angelic team is too busy to help out with your shopping list, think again. I have come to learn to state my intentions and shopping needs in advance of the actual trip to the store. If I make my list and trust in the divine, I will shortly there after hear when it is the right day to go shopping and will even be guided down the right aisles of the store. In this fashion, I have secured books by particular authors, denim jeans down to my favorite size and brand, and even specific and unique household items on my wish list.

My angelic team is always at work finding the most efficient routes along my path of life, even when it comes to driving. Oftentimes, I will get a nudge to turn off on a street I had not intended to go, only to stumble across a unique shop or to discover I had narrowly avoided an accident or traffic jam. Other times, I will get the urge to stop in at a favorite store even on a day I am running a little behind. On one particular occasion, I took a detour on the way to work. The detour was in response to an inner nudge to stop in at my favorite bookstore even though I had no intention of buying a book. When I arrived, I walked down a few aisles wondering why I had been guided to make the impromptu visit. Immediately after I posed the question, I rounded the corner and bumped into an old friend I had not seen in years. I had, however, been thinking about her just the day before and was wishing we could reconnect. Sometimes these chance encounters are needed on my part, and sometimes I am guided in a specific direction because a dear friend is the one who needs the encounter. Either way, it is always divinely orchestrated.

I am already a self-professed bird lady, so I am sure the notion that feathers bring angelic messages will be of no surprise. Feathers always show up in the strangest places on the days I most need to hear from my angelic team. For example, one of the many times in my life when I was questioning my healing experiences and purpose in this world, the tiniest little white feather floated down from the heavens and landed right on my lap. The unique part of this story is that I was inside my home sitting on the couch. And no, we do not have anything in our house that is down-filled. Now you can take from this story what you will, but the important part about welcoming spirit into your life, is to gratefully accept these small gifts and gestures, never doubting the messages are provided by the spirit world as reassurance of their presence. To do so, is to live a blessed life.

Other times feathers are found right where you would expect them to be within nature. However, it is how and when they are found that signifies a divine messenger was involved. One time I was walking along a trail and talking with spirit, asking a question about my life's path as a healer. In response to my question as I looked to the sky for answers, I was guided to instead look down. There at my feet was a beautiful feather. To me the feather symbolizes our connection with the divine and their infinite presence in our lives. These small gifts are used from the heavens to confirm we are on the right path and protected in all that we do. Message received.

11:11 is my magical number. It is a silent encouragement I receive from my angelic cheering section. To me, the number represents new beginnings and my dreams quickly manifesting into reality. The number confirms I am on the right path and making the right decisions. What I have learned to recognize is that I am always guided to look at the clock at just the right moment to witness this supportive message from above. In fact, I was just sitting here wondering what "short but sweet" experience I should write about next, when I was guided to look at the clock to find my answer, and there it was again, 11:11.

Speaking of clocks, I also had an encounter with an antique clock. This masterfully crafted timepiece belonged to my grandpa and grandma. I inherited the clock years later after my grandparents had already passed. The actual clock does not work anymore. Over the years, it has received many tune-ups. However, the hands no longer move and the chime no longer works. No matter how many times we wind the clock, it will stop once it reaches 4:00. That being said, the clock is still proudly displayed in my kitchen, silently defying time. On one particular day, I was thinking about how everything always happens for a reason and everything in its own time. At that exact moment, the old clock began to chime. In fact, it chimed ten times while the hands stood firmly at 5:00. Never before and never again have I heard the clock chime or witnessed the hands move. However, I look forward to the day I do. For I will know my dear friends from the spirit world are once again providing confirmation to my timely thoughts.

Physical aliments in our body are also a gift and message from spirit, although most of our society does not perceive them as such. Physical aliments come into our lives as a navigational tool. If we listen, our bodies will point us in the right direction, help us create balance in our lives, and keep us from veering from our path. Many of the aches and pains we endure as humans are just road signs. It took me many years to understand the navigational system of my body. However, once I understood the language, life became a lot easier.

Activating your SOULworks

Spirit is all around and within us. We are spirit. We are all-powerful souls of the light, here on earth to have a human experience. Our angels and guides are always by our side, and always willing to lend us a helping hand. Even if you have not personally experienced or recognized spiritual encounters, your angelic team is always working behind the scenes for you. Learn how to listen with new ears, view the world with new eyes, and hold a belief in your heart amplifying an acceptance of a world that is much greater than what initially meets the eye. Believing in the unknown opens your awareness, provides clarity to your perceptions, and increases your sensitivity to the spirit world. In doing so, you will start to notice an increase in the vibrancies of color and the energy that is all around and within you.

There are infinite ways spirit will communicate with us here on earth. The possibilities are only limited to your own mind. In fact, encourage your spirit guides to provide proof of their existence. Open your awareness by believing in their presence and then actively watch for their signs. Once you receive a sign, give thanks. Avoid the impulse to dismiss the encounter as mere chance. It is in those small but mighty moments when spirit truly shines, and reveals their infinite commitment and involvement in our lives. Once this bond is recognized, there will be no limit to what your combined light force can achieve. So, let's get started.

Your Move:

☐ **Establish your thing.** Ask your spirit guides to show you a sign of their existence and ever presence in your life. Keep your mind open. My thing is strategically placed birds. However, your sign can be any number of things. Once established, trust that every time your sign enters your life, your spirit guides are supporting you. Also, establish a sign to show you are on the right path. I utilize 11:11 or 111 for this purpose. Again, your sign will be personalized and have meaning to you. Perhaps it is color, music, animals or symbols; the possibilities are endless. Trust in the information received and acknowledge your guides anytime your sign presents itself.

☐ **Respond.** Signs provided by spirit are like sign posts along your journey. If you are pondering a positive change in your life and receive confirmation from spirit to move forward, please take their advice. Standing idol never creates change. Do not be the person who complains that nothing in their life ever changes, and yet are afraid to make the first move when an opportunity presents itself.

☐ **Trust in your inner wisdom.** Your higher self is just as capable of providing guidance as your angelic team. In fact, we are all energetically connected. Go within your heart and listen for signs and messages from your inner self. Move forward with your gut feelings and instincts. Trust you are where you are supposed to be in life and strive to enhance your experience. Your path can be as exciting and successful as you desire, so dream big.

☐ **Enjoy the small things in life.** Life is grand when you take the time to enjoy yourselves and those around you. Live in the present and cherish every moment here on earth. Watch for the magic and divine inspirations that are all around you. Many small and precious experiences will produce more nourishment for your soul than a handful of one-time events. Take inventory of your life-defining moments, small and large. Give thanks for your life and the divine light within us all.

CHAPTER 12

Home Sweet Home

My family lives in a century-year-old home that has actually been on four different homesteads miles apart. Of course, nowadays, people move houses all the time. However, the first three locations our house called home were all prior to the 1970's, meaning some of those moves were even accomplished by horse and buggy. No small feat for a two and a half storey structure made of lath and plaster. Despite its grand history, the actual house is neither grand nor large. It is a simple old farmhouse that has stood the test of time and continued to shelter family after family, and renovation after renovation for one hundred years. The few years just prior to my family purchasing the house was the only time the house actually stood empty. Otherwise, this house has always provided a loving home.

My husband and I moved the abandoned house in 2003 and have spent years restoring and refurbishing inside and out. It has taken a lot of sweat, hard work, frustration, and dedication to bring life back into the old nostalgic house. Throughout our work, there was always evidence of angelic support during this large undertaking. However, sometimes it took a bit of time to recognize it as such. One time in particular, I remember working on the wiring for the upstairs hallway. I had run the wires three times and had failed miserably every single time I tried. Each attempt ended in despair; whether the wires were too short, structural obstacles were in the way, or the wires were accidentally drilling through, the results were always disastrous. When I had reached my final breaking point, I called my husband for assistance and we both stood there in the hallway looking up at my troubles. It was then we realized the entire area should have been bypassed entirely, so we could make room for a future access door to the attic. If I had managed to wire the area, we would have surely regretted it down the road. Of course, I have no doubt my angels already knew our future plans for the attic, and were creatively trying to get my attention to avoid running the wires in the first place.

That was not the last time the spiritual world pitched in. Like most renovations, a lot of photos where snapped along the way charting our progress. We had two areas of our house that we found most challenging, the back entry and the porch. The scale of the development was large and a little out of our scope and comfort zone for mere weekend renovators. Looking back on the photos there are orbs of light that appear in each of these locations. I believe our spirit guides hung around very closely during those tough times to help us through. And of course, we did make it through each project step by step until the old abandoned farmhouse became our home.

Once the house was finished, our interactions with the spirit world did not stop there. The next encounter occurred in the middle of a winter night while I was sleeping. While deep in slumber, I was dreaming I was wandering downstairs in the middle of the night to fetch a glass of water. When I arrived in our newly renovated kitchen, I was greeted by the unexpected presence of three adult spirits sitting at my kitchen table. Startled, I asked what they were doing in my house. They responded they had found the front door wide open and decided to come on in to see how our renovations were coming along. They even complimented my kitchen, saying they loved what my family had done to the place. We did not introduce ourselves, but instinctively I knew they were folks who had lived in the house prior to us.

In the morning, I headed down to the kitchen as I mulled over the dream from the night before and its possible meanings. The vision had felt so real, like I had really travelled down to the kitchen to talk to the visitors in the night. My thoughts were quickly interrupted as I rounded the stairs and stopped in my tracks. The front door to our house was standing wide open, just as the spirits had indicated.

Upon closer investigation, I realized the door had not latched properly and the windy night had blown the door wide open. At the time, I did not doubt for one minute the friendly past occupants of our house had come to visit and my dream was a mere glimpse of the events. It was later when I became more aware of my dream walking, that I also realized my own spirit would have also travelled down the stairs that night to greet my guests and converse about our renovation. After all, what kind of hostess would I be if I had not.

The building of our home has been an integral part of my journey. It has taught me to dream big, move into the unknown, and to push myself beyond what I originally thought was possible. In that determination and blind faith, we created our home.

So why do I speak of a home in a book about healing? The energy in each person's home is different. It is a collection of their belongings, hopes, dreams, and experiences. A home can be healing if it is where your heart is. Some homes have a lot of heart. These are the ones you feel instantly comforted by the minute you walk in the door. Have you experienced this phenomenon? It is like the energy rushes to greet you with a big welcoming hug.

I feel this divine energetic hug from the heavens every time I enter my home. The atmosphere is relaxing, calming, inviting, and serene. I can literally feel the warmth and love that comes from the spirit within my home. As you become more aware of spirit, you will notice this feeling is always present within Mother Nature. However, when you open your heart and invite spirit into your home, you can also feel this divine energy within.

I realize I am biased towards my own home, but others feel it too. People who visit our place always express their joy and good feelings received from our home. Their health and spirits improve. They feel safe and comfortable. Many report not even wanting to leave. I believe this surge of energy is a combination of the history of our home, the love that has been poured into it for generations, the open hearts of those who reside within, and our welcoming attitude towards spirit. Spirit has been invited into our lives and into our home; the feeling of this divine love is literally tangible.

There has only been one other house in my life (so far) that conjured up these similar feeling; it was my Grandma Annie's home. There was always an overwhelming sense of love, comfort, and security just by being there. It felt like a mixture of homemade cookies, hugs, and support all at once, even when sometimes there physically were none. In fact, whenever it was time to leave grandma's place, my dad used to have to carry me out kicking and screaming. As a child, I could not even explain the attraction, but there was so much warmth and love in that house and I never wanted to leave. I could have just stayed there forever soaking up the good vibes and energy. Looking back, I believe the energy of that house was achieved in a similar fashion to mine; an open heart, mind, and soul to those who reside within.

Activating your SOULworks

Creating a welcoming home does not take a lot of money or material possessions. It takes heart. Regardless of whether you reside in a temporary lodging or your dream home, you have the ability to increase the vibrational energy and make your space feel comfortable and welcoming. To do so, will help improve your own well-being and the experiences of all who enter. Living within good energy will improve your health and keep you in a more positive state of mind. When you consider your home from this perspective, you really cannot afford not to spend the time and effort to improve your dwelling.

Even on a small scale you can see the logic and effects behind positive energies within a space. Walking into a messy or cluttered room can leave you feeling overwhelmed. Entering a space where negativity abounds will dramatically decrease your own energy and positive outlook. If you continually feel disappointed or frustrated with your own living space, this energy will also flow into your life and those around you. On the flip side, creating a positive and pleasing space will enhance your world and the world around you.

Your Move:

- ❑ **Decorate from the heart.** Fill your home with the things you love. Do not worry so much about whether your belongings follow the current trends and fashions. Instead, focus on what truly makes your heart sing. Maybe it is a great bargain you found at a garage sale. Perhaps you have old furnishings or memorabilia from departed loved ones. Or perhaps it is a collection of artifacts you have gathered along your travels. Find the items and furnishings you are really drawn to and bring them into your house. What will add true interest and warmth to your home is a collection of valued items. Not valuable in monetary terms, but valuable to your heart. Make these changes to your home and then notice the shift in energy.

☐ **Feel the love.** Experiment with energy. Walk into different areas of your home and notice the differences in the way you feel. Which room brings you the most comfort? The art of Feng Shui is all about creating positive energy and affecting the vibrations under your roof. However, you do not have to be an expert in the art of Feng Shui to notice the feel of a room. Simply hold the intention to notice. Expand your scope by taking your experiment on the road. Feel the difference in energy when you enter someone else's home, your place of work, a public building, outdoors or a spiritual dwelling. What space provides the most positive feelings? Can you feel the divine energy and empowerment? Does the space give you the impression God is reaching down from the heavens and hugging you at that very moment? If so, what elements are present within this location that may be missing from others?

☐ **Welcome spirit.** To truly raise the vibration of a home, welcome spirit into your dwelling with open arms. Ask your angels to always be present within the walls of your place and also outside your home at all times. Request the presence of your spirit guides and departed loved ones. Ask for their help to increase the energy within your home for the greatest good of you and everyone who enters. Always hold the intention to keep the energy within your home, place of work, and any buildings you frequent, positive and full of light. Envision the universal light coming down from the heavens and surrounding your home and your possessions. Do not be afraid to interact with these beings of the light. Treat them as the valued guests they are.

❑ **Consciously create.** Perhaps you do not currently reside in the home of your dreams or have a large renovation project ahead of you. Start to visualize successfully attaining your goals. For renovations, work on one project at a time and request the help from various spirit guides who are experts in the field. You do not have to know who is an expert in the field, simply request that the perfect light being from the spirit world to come and help with your project. If you are searching for the perfect home, keep an open mind. Listen to your inner wisdom and keep an open eye for signs. Also, do not feel compelled to beat the Jones. Understand that a small home can have more heart and positive energies than even the grandest of mansions. Consciously focus on attaining a feel-good home, regardless of size, location or possessions held within.

❑ **Health and home.** Start noticing where you want to be when you feel sick. Is it at home on the couch? Curled up in your own bed? Back at your folks' place? Over at grandma's? Perhaps at work? When our spirits are down, we will intuitively move to a location that is comfortable and provides security. Also, start to notice if your health improves or declines in certain locations. Become sensitive to the changes in your body by paying attention to your responses. If no place provides comfort, strive to make a change. Your health depends on it.

CHAPTER 13

Divine Planning

I have studied many schools of thought on life, death, and past lives. My beliefs stem from my experiences and are also confirmed by similar findings from others who work with the spirit world. I will start this chapter by sharing a few scenes in my life and then wrap it up with an overview of my position on the divine plan of life.

Past Lives

Over the years, I have had many experiences confirming the existence of past lives. Not only do we carry emotional and physical baggage ahead with us into this lifetime, we also carry knowledge and memories. My first encounter with this concept occurred before I had given any thought to the topic or read any resources on the subject. In fact, I had grown up in a family where past lives and reincarnation were not even considered possible. Furthermore, they were not discussed.

At the age of three my daughter had an imaginary friend, or at least that is what society likes to call childhood visitations from the spirit world. On one particular day, I passed my daughter's bedroom and overheard her talking to someone. I only heard my daughter's side of the conversation, but there were definite pauses in the discussion while she eagerly awaited the response of her guest. Puzzled, I peaked in the doorway and asked who she was talking with. Her response was immediate with no hesitation or thought. She merely replied, "I am talking to my mom. You know, the one I had before I came here to have you as a mom."

Did she just say what I think she did? Wow, the wheels were turning in my mind and the idea of past lives began to blossom in my world.

—◀▶—

Death

I have come to believe no matter how devastating death can be to those left behind, it is always a planned event on a soul level. Once again, my experience with the concept of planned deaths occurred prior to any thought or research conducted on the topic.

To explain my views on divinely designed death, I need to set the scene. Years back while in high school I had a particular experience with my grandparents. I had just arrived at school but was feeling rather ill. Instead of staying in class, I decided to walk to my grandparent's house only a few blocks away to lie down and rest. When I arrived, both grandpa and grandma were still sound asleep, so I made myself at home, quietly crawling onto their couch and dozing off. I am not sure how long I had been there, but I did wake up and realize my grandparents were no longer sleeping but instead standing between the living room and kitchen. Neither one had realized I was there and to my youthful disgust they were kissing. In a panicked and embarrassed state, I quickly closed my eyes and pretended to sleep. Then I heard my grandma say "Oh, Lauren is here," and on that cue, I opened my eyes and officially woke up.

Fast-forward many years. My grandpa was suffering from Parkinson's disease and had been transferred to long-term care. The prognosis on his health was not good and everyone knew it was just a matter of time. One night I had a very peculiar premonition about his passing. The dream was so vivid I woke up with a start, remembering every detail.

In the dream, I was lying down on that very same couch in grandpa and grandma's house. My grandparents were standing in the same location as before, however the only way I recognized them was because the layout was identical to the actual event years earlier. Unlike the first version, this time my grandparents were young and vibrant. Their appearance actually replicated photos I had seen of them in their early thirties. In the vision, they were discussing death, but it was not like anything I had ever heard before. They were actually planning what age they would be when they died and who would return to heaven first. I distinctly remember grandma requesting to return to heaven prior to her husband. She was adamant this was her preference, and grandpa reluctantly agreed, but promised he would not be very far behind. Then, just as it had occurred so many years before, my grandma noticed I was witnessing their conversation. Once again, she declared "Oh, Lauren is here," and on that note, I woke up from my dream.

To my earthly mind, the dream did not make much sense at the time. Grandpa was the one with health problems and grandma was still as vibrant and active as she had ever been. I also had no frame of reference to attribute the planned discussions on death. Suicide came to mind, but that did not make much sense in the case of my grandparents. My only response was to dismiss the dream altogether. Six weeks later my mom phoned with the news of my grandma's passing. After 80 years of living here on earth and with no previous health condition at all, her heart simply stopped. Exactly

80 days after her death, my grandpa, also at the ripe age of 80, gracefully passed away, joining my grandma in heaven exactly as he had promised so many years before. Like a modern day Romeo and Juliet, these two wonderful souls planned their destiny, lived life to its fullest, and then gracefully exited together.

Combining these two experiences and many more years of similar events, I have come to the following conclusions as so many others have before me. We are souls here on earth living a human life. Before we incarnate on earth, we pick our soul group to whom we will interact, we select exit points where we have the opportunity to go back home to heaven, and we choose major life themes we wish to experience along the way, with the intention of learning and growing from these encounters. Our ultimate goal is to become enlightened here on earth and to lift the veil between our worlds. That being said, there is most certainly a divine plan in all we do.

Activating your SOULworks

Many people question the validity of past lives. To me, it is the only logical explanation to describe the workings of our soul. After all, can you really imagine a God who does not recycle? If you think earth is crowded, can you imagine centuries of souls in heaven with no reason or motivation to return to human form? With so many life lessons to learn and experiences to encounter, do you really choose to believe we would only take a crack at this thing we call life once? With all the divine order of nature and the seasons of time, does it really make any sense at all that humans would not replicate this natural flow of progression?

I like to compare our souls to the workings of a tree. Just as a tree can experience many seasons of time, so too do our souls. Similar to how a tree will continue to grow, expand its roots, and reach towards the heavens, so too will our inner beings. Externally, the years of growth may not be visible on a tree. However, if we look within, we can see the changes and experiences over time. The presence of evolution within the plant world is definitely traceable. In a similar fashion, if we take the time to look, we can observe the lifetimes of growth within our soul.

Within our life there also exists what we call soul groups. These are the people within our lifetime we choose to interact with. Before we come to earth, we select what type of family we will be raised in; the people who will come into our lives even for just a brief moment of time but leave a lasting impact on our souls; we even select those who will cause us hardships and challenges. In fact, those who cause us the greatest trouble are those at a soul level who are our best of friends. Our BFFs. Think about it. If we were going to designate someone to come into our lives, raise havoc, and teach us a very difficult life lesson, we would select someone we trusted and were very close to.

The potential and combination of experiences we have to encounter while here on earth are infinite and so too are our life lessons. However, like others have pointed out before me, there does seem to be prevailing categories that are predominately encountered. These themes can include topics such as financial, relationships, emotional, health, spiritual growth, leadership, racial, sexual orientation, confidence, and the list goes on. I also find any of these life experiences will continue to repeat over and over again until our soul learns and grows from the encounter. This continuation can be in one lifetime or over many.

Your Move:

- ❑ **Identify soul groups.** Have you ever met someone for the first time and immediately connected on a deeper level? Like you have literally known each other your entire life? Chances are you have, at a soul level. Think about all the people who have come into your life. Understand they are all a part of your journey for a reason. Identify people that swiftly entered and exited your life leaving a lasting impact. What lessons did they teach you? What part of your divine plan did they serve? Spend time contemplating your family tree. What type of family were you born into and how has it helped direct your life's journey? Give thanks for the many lessons everyone has brought into your life and the challenges they have created. It is these challenges and obstacles that strengthen your soul.

❑ **Connect with past lives.** Take some time to meditate on your past lives. What images come into your mind? What experiences are front and centre? Trust in the information you receive and use this knowledge to help with future endeavors. Ponder any fears or health problems you currently have in this lifetime that seem unjustified. Ask your inner self where the problems stem from. If the memories are brought forward from past lives, thank your higher self for the experience. Then ask to have your physical connection to them lifted.

❑ **Recognize life lessons.** Take a close look at your life and the lessons you have learned. What seems to be the overall theme? Strive to forgive the tough lessons in your life and thank your higher self for the experiences encountered. Is there one area in your life that continues to draw energy? Review your largest obstacles and determine if there are any underlying messages or lessons. Ask your guides and angels to help you move forward.

CHAPTER 14

In Sickness and in Health

The overall health of our body is a matter of the soul. As I have already indicated, we are first and foremost a soul here on earth to experience life as a human. Furthermore, even while here on earth and regardless of the state of our health, our souls are always and will always be a perfect reflection of God. Regardless of how many imperfections our bodies may exhibit while here on earth, the true blueprint of our soul is unique, infinite, and flawless by design. In that truth, we are never alone in our struggles and we are never vulnerable to the unknown. Every person here on earth has the assurance of being greatly loved and protected by spirit, in both sickness and in health.

So why do we suffer from illness and disease while on earth? There are a number of causes affecting the state of our health. I have witnessed a number of scenarios and have grown to strongly believe almost all health problems can be overcome.

I will start with my own personal experience. I speak quite fluently about my journey of becoming an Intuitive Healer. What I have neglected to include in the story so far is the time when I was very ill. During this dark period of my life, it literally felt like death was knocking on my door. The list of medical issues plaguing my life was long and intensive with no seeming medical explanation. There were many visits to doctors and specialists trying to determine what had stopped my otherwise healthy body in its tracks. There were many educated guesses ranging from the onset of multiple sclerosis, to fibromyalgia, to widespread chronic pain, to depression. My family was concerned, I was frustrated, and the doctors were perplexed.

I have always believed most health problems come into our life when it is time for us to assess our situation and make room for a shift to occur. The key is to find the reason and move forward. In times of illness, we are often closed off from spirit and slightly off the charted course of our soul. The time provided during the healing process is a time for reflection. It is a time to look at our lives, listen to our hearts, and make necessary changes to our routines. For those who are closed off to spirit as I was at the time, health problems are sometimes the only way our higher self can get our attention. Our hearts are crying out and literally using our bodies as the megaphone. There are many great books out there demonstrating the correlation between health problems and emotional call outs from the heart and soul, so I will not go into the details here. To expand on this point, we only need to understand the concept of these emotional ties and learn to listen to our souls. In my case, the emotional call out was to start speaking my truth about my spiritual encounters, as well as to seek to understand their purpose in my life. By keeping all my stories and experiences to myself, I was living a lie; the more I kept it in, the harder my body worked to get my attention and release my truths. Once I realized this huge part of my life was missing from my everyday routine, my health started to improve. Once I acted upon this realization and started to study spiritual encounters and energy healing to validate and grow my awareness, my health blossomed. And once I stood in my power, spoke my truth, and feared no more, my life truly began.

Similarly, I also believe we come to earth with a few planned exit points. These points are times in our life when our soul can evaluate if we have achieved the tasks and lessons in life we set out to accomplish and make a decision to stay on earth or go back home (to heaven). Disease and illness are often used as an 'out' during these exit points. However, we do have the power within ourselves to acknowledge their purpose in our lives, surpass the health problems, and choose to stay here on earth. The choice is ultimately ours. An example of a planned exit point can be viewed in my original experience with my mom during her cardiac arrest. My mom was given a chance to review her life and make a decision to continue her life path here on earth or to journey home to heaven. Her choice was to stay, and I am forever grateful of her decision.

I have also witnessed many exit points where a decision was made to go home to heaven. My Grandma Annie was one of them. Her life came to a sudden halt with the onset of acute leukemia. Grandma's health quickly deteriorated from an active lifestyle to being on her deathbed within weeks. She knew it was her time to go and clearly indicated she would be in heaven by Easter morning. Although I instinctively knew her time was up as well, I did not want to say goodbye. She was my best friend and I could not imagine life without her. While sitting at her bedside the day before her passing, my grandma politely said it was time for me to head home, so I could be with my family. In my mind, I silently responded by arguing I did not want to leave her side because I intuitively knew she would be gone by morning. My grandma picked up on my concerns telepathically and then audibly responded, "even so, you should be with your family during this time. They will provide you comfort when I am gone". With that, I accepted her request. We said our emotional goodbyes and I left the hospital.

Although I was back at home with my family, my goodbye at the hospital would not be the last time I heard from grandma Annie before her passing. Later that night my grandma visited in spirit. She told me her time had come but she would always be with me. I tearfully said my final goodbye and accepted her decision to go back home to heaven. I checked the clock and it was not even midnight.

Later in my sleep, I had another vision. This time, I was remotely viewing my grandma's hospital room. In the room beside my grandma's bed were the spirits of my grandpa, my uncle (grandma's son), and my grandma's second husband, all who had journeyed to heaven before her. In the vision, I could clearly hear my grandma say, "Well it's about time you guys showed up!" And with that signature characteristic remark, my loved ones all laughed at her candor, took her by the hand, and gracefully welcomed her back home.

For the second time that night I woke, this time knowing my grandma had just taken her final breath. I looked at the clock; it was Easter morning. Peacefully, I dozed back to sleep knowing my grandma was where she wanted to be.

The third time I woke was not until morning and the sound of our phone ringing. I was not surprised to receive the news. My grandma had peacefully passed away. She had returned home on Easter morning, just as she had predicted nearly a month earlier. As the sun began to rise at the start of that wonderful and glorious day, one could not help but look up to the heavens and smile at yet another divine spirit who chose to rise again on Easter.

Yes, I grieved the passing of my dear grandma. However, there is so much comfort in knowing we are not victims of disease, but active participants in our growth and life transitions. My grandma had gracefully chosen her destiny at a soul level and I had witnessed her evolution. Her timely visit to my house in spirit was three hours prior to her actual death and confirmed her decision to freely leave her body behind. Not only did this provide my heart with reassurance and closure, it was also the first of many wonderful examples of how health problems, no matter how sudden or tragic, are used as a planned exit point to transition from this life into the next.

Health problems also come into our lives because they are a reflection of our past. The existence of past lives actually has a dramatic impact on the health of our body, mind, and soul. If there were unresolved issues in a past life, oftentimes we will bring these health conditions or traumatic events into the present. Although we may not remember past life traumas on a conscious level, sometimes they will start in this life where they left off in the past. Likewise, events in our current life can also trigger these memories at a specific age and then replicate or closely mimic the past circumstances. Once we are able to identify the cause and grow for the experience, we are also able to overcome the illness.

Another reason illness or disease enters our life is because we chose it as part of our divine plan. Every soul travels to earth with a purpose and lessons we want to experience in life. Sometimes this does include learning to overcome a disability or experiencing the pain and suffering caused by illness and disease. Only the strongest of souls choose this path. Although it is part of our soul journey, we may also choose to eventually overcome the obstacles within this lifetime. This scenario takes determination and dedication, but anything is possible to those who believe.

Lastly, we should not overlook the concept of manifesting the state of our health for not only ourselves, but also manifesting a positive state of health for all of society and Mother Earth. Our thoughts do in fact create our reality. Please pay attention to where your thought forms are focused. Are your thoughts centred on peace or destruction; abundance or scarcity; beauty or the lack of; wellness or disease?

Where your focus lies, your reality will also follow. Unfortunately, the bulk of society continues to spend the majority of their time thinking, talking, and fearing not only disease but also famine and destruction. My parents used to tell me if I did not have anything nice to say, then to not say anything at all. I would echo this advice on our thoughts. Trust in spirit and our ability to manifest an inspired life. We can and we will. Thanks be to God.

Activating your SOULworks

Looking at your health from a new vantage point is a wonderful way to become an active participant in your life's journey. Having the capacity and insights to view health problems as an opportunity, instead of a threat, is to take control of your life and move forward towards enlightenment.

I will give you an example to get you started. Not so long ago, I suffered a concussion that took nearly six months to recover from. Yes, it was a hard experience to endure, and yes there were times when my faith began to waiver.

During this time, I found it very difficult to be in crowds and could not handle being around any kind of noise. I also found it very difficult to think and carry out day-to-day activities that we all tend to take for granted. Life as I knew it ground to a halt. However, while suffering from the concussion, I also had the opportunity to go within. I could not be out in public, but I could spend hours alone in contemplation. It was during this time of reflection that I officially decided it was time to move into my SOULworks career full-time.

It was also during this time I discovered my intuitive abilities and sensitivities to energies had expanded. In fact, I would describe them as quadrupled after the concussion. I took this as a sign to move forward on the path of an Intuitive Healer. (As a complete side note, since my trauma, I have come to the conclusion that many people who suffer concussions experience heightened sensitivity to the energy fields around them. They just may not be aware of these enhanced intuitive abilities because they have no frame of reference from which to compare them. I, on the other hand, was already talking to the deceased, experiencing visions, and sensing others' energy fields. The concussion notably increased these sensitivities and it took six months to adjust to the expanded abilities).

During the concussion, I also found it difficult to work on the computer, watch television or read documents. However, I could practice healing techniques and send healing to those in need. In fact, sending healing energy was the only activity I did not find overwhelming. I took this as another sign to move forward.

What started as a threat soon began to blossom into an opportunity - an opportunity I had even asked for. You see, prior to the concussion I was already becoming very aware of the spiritual changes occurring within me. I knew I was being called to be an Intuitive Healer full-time and was confident in my ability to do so. However, I could not imagine how I would transition from my career in marketing to a life of spiritual healing and teaching. Unable to proceed on my own, I decided to hand my situation over to the Powers that Be. I clearly declared my intentions of becoming a full-time Intuitive Healer. If that was my life purpose, I asked them to provide me a space in which to transition. I asked for an opportunity that would enable a graceful leave from my current place of work, an opportunity that would allow me the time to prepare. I also asked for an opportunity that would not affect my family financially and would also help my family understand my aspirations to becoming a spiritual healer. Upon closer inspection, all my requests had been answered miraculously through the concussion. Once I recognized my head injury as my requested transition point, my health began to improve and everything just started falling into place.

The day I hit my head I saw stars. Looking back, I believe they were the stars intended to guide my life and help me along my journey. Keep your mind open and your eyes peeled for the moments in your life that miraculously demonstrate the grace of God and a fork in the road to your development. Always trust you are being cared for. Remember to view both sides of the story and accept there is a larger divine plan we are not always privy to.

Your Move:

- ❏ **Look for opportunities.** Take the time to review any major illnesses that have entered your life. Think about what opportunities occurred or had the potential to occur because of the health problems. Look at the state of your current health. Do you have any persistent ailments? If so, take a moment to listen to you body. Ask what message your higher self is trying to tell you. Follow your heart and trust in the answers you receive.

- ❏ **Review experiences with death.** Reconsider any past deaths of family members and friends. Were there any signs or messages prior to their death that reflected the upcoming exit point? Know that on a soul level all exit points are chosen. Does this change the way you feel about their untimely death? Try to see their death as a celebration and transition into the next stage of their soul's path.

- ❏ **Manifest health.** Review your thought patterns regarding hereditary disease in your family. Do you have a tendency to blame health problems on your ancestors? Do you assume your health will follow the same pattern of a loved one even though you currently have no symptoms? Society has a tendency to manifest disease merely because we believe we are destined to develop it. In this manner, we are actually creating our reality. Instead of sending fear of disease into your life, surround yourself in healing energy, listen to the messages your body is trying to convey, and then release your worries to the heavens.

❏ **Listen to the hidden wisdom.** Do you or a loved one currently suffer from a terminal illness? Take the time to honor your soul and the journey you have endeavored to take. Reflect on the lessons this hardship has brought you. Look for the positive within the pain. Has the disease brought your family closer? Has it increased your spiritual awareness? Does the disease represent something in your life you need to let go of or change? Listen closely and grow from this experience. Only the strongest of souls would ever have chosen a path so difficult.

CHAPTER 15

Think Responsibly

I would like to expand on the concept regarding our thoughts creating our reality. There is no one person living on earth that does not have a negative thought from time to time. It is a natural part of our human existence to have this shadow side. In fact, I believe our ego began the minute we separated from Source energy. This monumental day is symbolized in the story of Adam and Eve; when mankind moved towards being individuals and less comprised of one glorified unit of spirit. Since that time, there has been an over-riding balance existing in the world depicted in the equation of positive and negative, yin and yang, darkness and light.

The problem with our shadow side is that negativity hurts all involved; the originator, those who are close to the person being negative (either by actual proximity or relations), and ultimately our world. In this, I am not speaking of those who only exhibit radically negative behavior, as this is more the exception than the norm. What I am referring to is how often everyday people have negative thoughts and feelings, and how these internalized expressions are silently lethal. I know this to be true. I can literally feel negativity. I have grown to recognize the presence of this force and understand its power to run havoc on our health, both physically and emotionally.

Everyone has felt this truth to some extent. There is always an internal knowing when you walk into a room where a fight or argument has just taken place. The negative energy in the room will be dense and have a distinctive unpleasant feeling. This energy can bring your spirits down even on the brightest of days; and for the sensitive people out there, it can even make you feel physically sick. I have personally witnessed and experienced this phenomenon on countless occasions.

One particular situation involved my own health. I have been plagued with daily headaches my entire life. For years I visited specialists, carefully monitored my diet, and actively avoided common triggers trying to determine a cause to stop the relentless pounding. Recently the headaches have lessoned greatly. These changes began when I started working from home. What I found during this transition was astonishing. While in my own space on a regular basis my headaches would literally vanish. However, if I had a personally bad day where my emotions were running wild, if someone negative would enter my space or if I would venture out into a hectic public setting, my headaches would again ramp up until a full-blown headache was underway.

At first I attributed this phenomenon to stress and my strong desire to open my SOULworks business. Clearly, I found it more peaceful to be at home working on my life's dream and my body was merely reciprocating in a positive fashion. However, despite the concentrated focus on my life's work, there were still days when my headaches would return. With the increased alone time during this period, I was clearly able to see the connection between other people and my own state of health. The headaches would only start when I was in close proximity to someone who was depressed, angry, fearful or going through a rough spell in their lives (and yes, this could include me). Without realizing, these people and their negative energy were literally causing me pain. Their problems, frame of mind, and energy fields were literally affecting my health.

We are all connected on a soul level. So, it does not surprise me to realize this strong correlation between our individual thoughts and the profound effects our thoughts have on those around us. However, do not for one minute think we are all just innocent victims of our circumstance or that everyone around you is the problem. Blame is not the answer. You must also take some responsibility for your own thoughts. Take a look at the energy you create. Is it always positive? I would never claim to always live in a positive state of mind; however, I am striving to achieve this ultimate state of enlightenment.

The first time I realized my own anger caused a ripple affect out into the world was experienced quite innocently with my daughter. She was around the age of nine and having a wonderful day playing and having fun. My day was not quite as successful. I was having a miserable time working on a project I considered disastrous. I was mad, frustrated, and angry at the world. As I watched my daughter having a wonderful time in her youthful uncomplicated state, my anger only grew. Although I did not verbalize my frustrations, inside I was fuming. "It must be nice to be so young and carefree," I thought to myself, as I angrily continued on with my day.

Then I started to notice my daughter's demeanor change. What started as a wonderful day of play, quickly moved to sadness and gloom. Within one hour she was lying on the couch complaining of being tired and not feeling very good. Mad at this new development in an already miserable day, I crossly asked what had changed to make her feel so bad. When she failed to provide an answer, I flippantly suggested she go to bed so I could move on with my exasperated day.

Slowly, I began to realize the effects of my actions, and began to question the connection between my raging temper and my daughter's rapid decline in enthusiasm. Had my anger caused her day to veer sideways too? Had my enraged mood literally made her sick? Upon this new line of thinking, I pulled myself together and tested my suspicions. Silently I began to change my own attitude. I started to exude positive energies instead of negative. I began to smile, enjoy the project I was working on, and projected a more loving demeanor. Within minutes my daughter smiled with newfound energy. Merrily she confirmed feeling much better, and on that note she jumped off the couch and ran out to play.

The old adage is true: like attracts like. To expand on this truth, even in thought form, negative energy creates negative results and positive energy creates positive results. No matter what type of energy we are generating, it will always ripple out into the world and affect those around us. I wish I could say most people focus on positive thoughts, but I have learned this is not usually the case. Even the most positive person on the outside can store a lot of negative energy within.

Sometimes this irritated energy is even audible and I am able to hear glimpses of people's thoughts. The first time this occurred I was both startled and perplexed. I was standing in a line up waiting to pay for a jug of milk when a teenage girl walked by. Her lips did not move a muscle, but I distinctly heard her demanding request "get the hell out of my way, lady. God, I hate when people block this aisle." Shocked at her reaction to my seemingly harmless location in the cue, I looked around to discover I was in fact blocking an aisle. She had not spoken a word, but her thoughts had been audible just the same.

Similar experiences continued. Ironically at one time I believed I only had access to negative thoughts. After all, judgments, criticisms, anger or disapproval were primarily the only information I was receiving. Then the sad realization dawned on me, I do not have exclusive access to negative thoughts, people's thoughts are more often than not exclusively negative.

As we become more enlightened and back to our true identity of being one with God, our ego will eventually be eliminated. In the mean-time, the more enlightened we become, the more our shadow side will also move into survival mode in an effort to balance this earthly equation. Do not give in to this internal struggle. Many self-help advocates speak to the importance and magnitude positive thinking has on your life. Please heed this advice and begin to live in a more positive state of mind; your health and the health of all those around you depends on it. Actively become aware of your thoughts and make a conscious effort to think responsibly. Acknowledge the strong negative feelings you may feel towards particular people or situations, but then strive to see the true reflection of light and spirit within each. In doing so, your own inner light will shine.

Activating your SOULworks

Negativity breeds negativity. This is not a new concept. Society has discussed, and to some point, grasped this reality for eons. Certainly, in the workplace this is a common realization. Once water cooler talk escalates to gossip and negativity, the entire atmosphere of the building will change. The more people that get involved, the harder it is to escape this negative attitude. Many workplaces strive to eliminate this type of behavior head on. They understand how negativity can be contagious and harmful to the environment.

More and more people have also started to become more conscious of how our negative behavior and thoughts help to shape our own reality. Thanks to the growing awareness and increased resources on the subject matter, people are starting to understand we create our own existence and can manifest our deepest desires. However,

I feel most people still do not entirely understand the full scope and effects of negativity. What is missing from the equation is how our negativity, judgment or ridicule, even when only verbalized internally, has the power to affect those around us.

Most people find it difficult to maintain a positive outlook all the time. Whether they are feeling down on themselves, a co-worker or someone else in the community, our minds tend to wander away from affirmative thoughts to a more destructive zone of belittling and scorn. As a society, we have lived this way for centuries and change will not occur overnight. However, we can strive to change our ways and become a more positive influence on the world. We can strive to approach our world with more love, light, and understanding.

Your Move:

- ❑ **Be alert.** Pay attention to your thoughts and the effects they have on yourself and others. The next time you find yourself having a bad day, notice how your poor luck continues to snowball. Notice how your anger only adds to the problem and helps to create more difficulties. Start to also pay attention to the way your attitude affects those around you. The next time you come home or go to work in a super bad mood, notice the changes that occur to those who are within close proximity to you. Was everyone in a better mood before you arrived? Did your negative energy and thought forms bring the entire room down? Chances are, it did. Accept this truth and make a commitment to yourself to change your outlook and create a more positive energy shift. Purposely intend to have a better outcome. Send additional light and love into the situation. Ask your guides and angels to help ensure a positive outcome. Watch the positive changes that begin to occur in your life.

❑ **Experiment.** Take your positive energy out on the road. Notice how becoming outwardly more positive, smiling more, and keeping your thoughts pleasant affect even complete strangers. Without speaking one word, try to change the attitudes and outlook of those around you. Also, observe your negative energy and the swath of destruction it can leave behind. Establish how both positive and negative attitudes are contagious, and notice how a positive outlook creates more positive results. The next time you recognize someone near you has a headache, stomach ache or is just feeling off, double check your energy vibe and ensure all thought forms are positive. If your thoughts were negative, depressed, or moody in anyway, accept your contribution to their current state of health and change your attitude. Observe as changes begin to occur right before your eyes.

❑ **Expand your scope.** Once you understand the power of positive thoughts, expand your repertoire. The more positive thoughts, words, and deeds you put out into the universe, the more positive results you will get in return. Give it a try; I dare you. Provide an extra dose of kindness to a stranger. Pay a nice compliment to someone. Become more accepting of those who are different than you regardless of race, sexual orientation, financial status, religion or well-being. Take the time to put your good vibe on before entering someone else's environment, always ensuring you are in fact putting your best foot forward.

❑ **Send in the light.** There will no doubt be many situations you will encounter in your life, when those around you are suffering or life is just not going your way. It is within these moments that we have the greatest potential to make an energetic shift and contribution to the world around us.

Instead of sending hate vibes, worry or judgment towards the situation, send in the light. Visually imagine surrounding the entire situation and all people involved with universal energy. Do not doubt your role and abilities to change the outcome even for one moment. There is nothing you will encounter while here on earth that a positive dose of love and light will not help. Here are a few examples:

○ Is your boss or your spouse's boss causing stress? Take the high road by sending light and love to the situation. Surround the work environment, all co-workers, clients, and customers with good vibes. Trust it will work out for the best.

○ Is your child being bullied at school? Do not send hatred towards the bully or worry towards your own child. Instead, energetically send both children love and light from the heavens. Ask the guides and angels of both children to help resolve the situation with grace and ease.

○ Is someone in your life achieving more personal success than you are? Do not send resentment or jealous thoughts out into the world. Instead, acknowledge what you can learn from this individual's success and send blessings to you both. Wish them continued achievements and give a heartfelt thank you for all of your own accomplishments. Trust in the divine order of all things.

○ Is a loved one suffering from an illness or emotional trauma? Do not send them worry or pity. Even when it comes from the heart, worry is energetically negative. To worry is to not trust in the divine order of all things. Take a more positive approach. Encompass the situation with positive thoughts. Visualize all things working out as per the divine plan and life lessons of all involved. Visualize the universal light providing positive reinforcements and ensuring a blessed outcome. Believe in the power of your thought forms and trust you are making a difference.

❏ **Give yourself a break.** Not everyone is perfect all the time. Everyone will have a bad day from time to time and our negative thoughts will not change over night. If you notice your thoughts are negative, give yourself a pat on the back. Noticing your thought patterns and actively striving to change for the positive is a step in the right direction. At least you are becoming aware of your thoughts. So many people blindly move through life without even realizing the impact they are making on their world and those around them. So, give yourself a break and celebrate your success. Continue to monitor your thoughts throughout the day and observe what situations cause your anxiety to escalate. Actively strive to change your outlook and outcome. Do your best to make improvements on your mood and thoughts one day at a time.

CHAPTER 16

A Miracle Defined

O n some occasions, I have been asked to help heal someone who is terminally ill. The call for help comes from all kinds of sources. Sometimes it is from the person themselves or from spirit, but more often than not it is from a loved one who is grasping to help a family member or friend. I do call myself an Intuitive Healer, but what I really do is provide a space to help facilitate a positive change within the body, mind OR soul. I have had to learn the hard way that even though a healing takes place, physical changes in the body are not always achieved.

Sometimes the healing is to help a person let their inner light grow stronger, their connection with the divine increase, and their fears and angers be removed so that they may peacefully go back home to heaven. It can also be to help the family through this hard time; to help them see that our souls continue to thrive on forever, even when our earthly bodies cease to exist.

On the flip side, healing is also used to help those who are sick listen to the messages their body is trying so desperately to get across, to help them to release any emotions that are keeping them from healing, and then to watch miracles happen. I have had the privilege of working with both scenarios, and either way, it is always an honor to be a part of this transition.

One transition I will always remember and hold near and dear to my heart involves the mother of a friend. The mother, who I will call Thelma, had been diagnosed with cancer and had rapidly moved into the status of terminally ill. Her family had been notified and all that was left to do was wait and pray. It was at that point that I was contacted and asked to offer my support to the family.

When I first reached out to my friend, I gave her some background information on my SOULworks and offered to visit her and her family. I explained a healing can take place on many different levels and I was not sure what the outcome would be. Even with the unknown, my offer was gratefully accepted and I was on my way.

While travelling to the hospital, I was given a number of visions and the word "Miracle" kept resounding through my mind, both of which made me feel fairly confident that a miracle would in fact be taking place. When I arrived, I was drawn to a garden area near the hospital. The trees and bright flowers calmed my nerves and offered a place of rest while I pulled myself together for the afternoon's session. While sitting in the garden, I saw a vision of my friend sitting on the bench thinking about her mom. It was not a sad setting. There were tears of joy streaming down her face. While leaving the garden I also noticed a plaque dedicating this tranquil area to cancer survivors. "Another good sign," I thought to myself as I confidently walked through the doors and into the corridor of the hospital.

At the bedside of this wonderful lady, I had the privilege to channel energy while I shared some personal and uplifting stories with her and her daughters. Stories that gave the family hope and demonstrated how our souls live on forever. I encouraged the family to never give up and always believe that a miracle would happen. I also explained how we decide at a soul level when it is time to go home, reiterating that when our soul does make its final decision, we are to honor that decision no matter what the outcome.

I wish I could tell you everything that happened during my session, but there are no words to describe the visions I saw. I knew at the end of the day what Thelma's soul had chosen. I was apprehensive to share the decision, but then again, the family already knew it in their hearts. I did see the room fill with angels and spirit guides; the smile on Thelma's face confirmed my vision. Loved ones always come through to help someone transition. They are like a welcome home committee and they are just waiting on the sidelines for exactly the right moment to take you home. A ceremony I witnessed at the end, involved water being poured over Thelma's head. It was a true spiritual baptism that her soul will always wear like a badge of honor. It was the moment her body, mind, and spirit truly become one with God.

Once our session was completed, I said my goodbyes and exited the room to give the family their last moments together. What I realized when I left the hospital room that wondrous day, was that despite my earlier thoughts, it was Thelma's family that were the true cancer survivors who would carry forward with a new-found appreciation of life, and all the blessings that are all around them. It was Thelma's two daughters who would grow from having been a part of their mom's transition.

The experience had certainly been magical and yet my fear and ego still snuck in through the back door. On the way home, I started not only second-guessing myself but also the messages I had shared. I had spoken of miracles and spiritual encounters. I had shared uplifting stories and given the family hope. And yet despite all of my efforts, their mom would soon be leaving this world and journeying to another dimension. Where was the miracle in that? What would the two daughters think of me? Had I caused more harm than good?

When I arrived home, I found two emails in my inbox, one from each of Thelma's daughters. Thelma had peacefully crossed over to the other side and her daughters were not only relieved her pain and suffering had finally ended, but they were also grateful for the work I had done. I share with you the following lines from their messages:

> "I want to thank you so much for visiting mom. I truly believe your healing paved the way for her to continue her journey with a clear focus and a sense of relief. It was shortly after your visit that she began her final journey, and it was very obvious to me that she needed your help to get there. I will be forever grateful for what you did for her."

> "I believe a miracle happened, and I think you were what gave the space and freedom for it to occur."

A friend once told me that to be a true healer, I must become more comfortable with death. It was within that conversation I started to realize a healing is not always of the body, but could also include the mind and soul. That realization was life changing for me.

Once again, I had the opportunity to learn new insights, and this time it was from spending time with Thelma and her daughters. During my time with them, I kept hearing the word "miracle." To my earthly mind, a miracle represented a physical improvement of the body. From that day forward I realized miracles and healings are intertwined. They can both occur at any level, be it the body, mind or soul. I will always be grateful to this wonderful mother and daughter team for showing me the true meaning of miracle…to put it simply, a miracle is a divine intervention that brings one closer to God.

Activating your SOULworks

Sending someone healing energies while they are on their deathbed is similar to the respect and honor you would provide an injured athlete while helping them cross the finish line. It is a privilege to provide a helping hand to someone in need. However, there is often one difference between my analogies in today's society. There is often an overwhelming pride surrounding the moment an athlete crosses a finish line, a victory of doing one's personal best. When someone finishes a race, the crowd will applaud and celebrate the success. Spectators are supportive and cheer each athlete on until the very end.

Unfortunately, more often than not, death does not bring this same response. Death usually conjures up fear, grief, and a deep feeling of sadness or loss that can span over years. In fact, this sadness often creates a hole in the hearts of those left behind, leaving loved ones in utter despair.

However, I feel this response to death is unnecessary and is brought on by a misunderstanding of the divine process of All that Is. When a soul makes the decision to return home to heaven, it means they have accomplished everything they set out to achieve within this lifetime. They have learned the lessons within their divine plan, conquered their goals, and have counted their blessings. On a soul level, they have made the decision to go back home and we must respect that decision. When someone returns to heaven it should be a celebration. These brave souls have ventured to earth, completed their mission, and successfully graduated from the lessons learned. To these brave souls, I cheer and echo the words of Thelma's daughter: "Way to go. I am so very proud of you."

Oftentimes, brave souls will also opt to leave our earth in an effort to help those left behind, to increase our awareness, and fulfill our own

SOULworks. Loved ones will sacrifice their progress on earth so that others may learn from them at a faster pace, growing stronger as an individual, family, and society. This is often the case in large tragic events of destruction. To these brave souls, I also cheer: "Thank you for your contributions to our world. I look forward to working with you to help advance the souls of mankind. Your death will not be for naught."

Your Move:

❑ **Honor the deceased.** Give yourself permission to honor and celebrate the lives of loved ones who have passed before you. It is okay to grieve and dearly miss a beloved. However, also take the time to pay tribute to their life's work. Acknowledge their accomplishments. Give them the gift of love and sheer appreciation for the life they lead. Learn from their lessons. Recognize their struggles and downfalls. Observe their strengths and successes. Know that every detail of their life was on course with their divine will. Thank them for being a part of your SOULworks.

❑ **Send healing energy to the dying.** In truth, there is no death. Our souls continue on forever. However, for those who are already within their time of transition from here on earth, take the time to send them loving energy from your heart. Visualize their physical, emotional, and spiritual pains overcome. Hold the space for them to clearly recognize their divine self and the light they emanate from within. Be there for them in body, mind, and spirit as they cross the finish line of life on earth.

❑ **Continue to communicate.** All lives continue from the soul level even after we have transitioned from this world.

I encourage you to keep the lines of communication open between your loved ones, even after they have left this earth. Their soul still lives on, just in another dimension. Talk to your deceased loved ones; ask them to continue to be in your life. Include them in your day-to-day living. Personally invite them to your monumental moments in life such as a wedding day, birth of your child or birthday celebrations. Know that they will be there. Provide a place of honor within your home so you are always reminded of their presence. Ask them to be by your side during the good times and the bad. Talk to your deceased loved ones like they are there and are still an active part of your life, because they truly are.

❏ **Give the gift of a miracle.** A miracle is a divine intervention that brings one closer to God. You can be the miracle and help someone with his or her spiritual growth or to overcome fears. You do not need to push your ideas on anyone or force-feed them your beliefs. You only need to speak your truth and plant the seed of inspiration. Inspiration has the ability to move mountains and advance the soul. Be the miracle.

CHAPTER 17

It's a Girl

There was a time in my life not so long ago when I believed I was destined to have a third child within this lifetime. It is not because my husband and I were trying to expand our family or because I was having some deep desire to further my lineage; on the contrary, that was the furthest thing from my mind. In fact, I was quite content with my family of four and was happily entering the stage in my life when spiritual growth was my top priority. However, despite my opinions of a perfectly complete family, my thoughts of having a third child persisted. The thought patterns stemmed from interpretations I had made over a collection of odd and vivid dreams. These premonitions lasted for over three years and accurately predicated the birth of Anika.

My dreams started with my spirit guides asking that I prepare for the arrival of Anika. Never before that moment had I heard the name Anika, and to me it sounded divine. In fact, I purposely tucked it into the back of my memory banks, with the intention of sharing it with a friend of the family. Perhaps she would need it for the upcoming birth of her first child. But my spirit guides were very clear and adamant. They firmly stated I would be the one who needed to use the name and that she would be born September 2011. They asked me to believe in my ability to give birth to this change in my life and trust in her arrival. To my earthly mind, this could only mean one thing - a baby. And so, with this thought process underway, I started the long, drawn out, and emotionally turbulent times of continued messages and guidance regarding her birth.

I have learned over the years that messages will repeat themselves until we have accurately heard the intended meaning and have responded. I believe this is true. Although, interestingly enough, while you are in the thick of it, you often do not realize you have misinterpreted a message. Sure, I doubted my dreams regarding Anika's arrival and my ability to mother another child. However, the signs just kept right on coming.

The next dream involved a trip to the Akashic records. For those unfamiliar with the term, this is a spiritual library that holds all the workings of your soul: past, present, and future. And yes, it does exist. In this particular premonition, I travelled to this great knowledge base with my spirit guide to gather information about my destiny. When I arrived, I was shown a great tablet and on it was inscribed the words "Believe in Anika." My spirit guide was pointing to the tablet and pleading for me to wake up and hear the messages within.

The dreams continued. Every month I would be shown new insights and further proof that Anika would in fact become a part of my life. I was asked to prepare my mind for the task at hand. "Together you will inspire the world," I kept hearing over and over again. Well, perhaps not everyone would think it is inspiring to have a third and unplanned child in your late thirties, but I certainly did. I had even grown to accept this fate as my own, and started to seriously consider the possibilities of having another baby. Why else would I be shown this birth? Why else would I be asked to make room in my life for her arrival?

One day while having lunch, I sat beside a lady I had never met before. I noticed she was pregnant and so we started to talk. As our conversation continued, my heart began to flutter. Was this a divinely inspired message? Here I was sitting with a complete stranger sharing baby names we were fond of, and that was not the amazing part. The astounding part was her secret confession to her favorite name, Anika. She indicated this name was within her family and she can still remember her dad saying, "Here comes Anika" when the little girl would come bounding into the room. This complete stranger also talked about becoming pregnant at what she believed was the perfect time in her life. And on that note, our conversation ended. I have always believed people come into our life at just the right moment to share the exact messages we need to hear. This was no exception. My thoughts of an expanding belly grew.

Another night was followed by another dream. For the second time, I was taken back to the Akashic Records. This time, more words appeared on the tablet, "Believe in Anika. She is within you." Upon viewing the tablet, I quickly woke up with a start. She is within me? Already? Well, you better believe I bought myself a pregnancy test the very next day. In fact, I bought one every month for the next six months. I even visited my doctor and asked if I could possibly be pregnant even though the tests showed otherwise. Despite the negative pregnancy tests and assurance from the doctor that I was not bearing a child, the messages continued to no avail.

Once again, I journeyed to the Akashic records within a vision and was shown the large tablet of my future. This time, I was asked to look even closer and as I did my heart filled with light. Peering ever closer I saw the words, "Believe in Anika. She is within you. Anika is you." I woke with a start and began to piece together all of the continued messages from over the span of the last few years. Could it be the message kept repeating itself because I did not interpret the message correctly? Could it be that Anika is my higher self and her birth will be my rebirth?

I believe this to be true; it just took me a very long time to understand the message. Funny thing though, despite my lack of understanding, I was always preparing for my spiritual self to be reborn. The workings of my soul were already underway. My expanding awareness was already growing. And at one point along my journey, I finally received the message loud and clear. "Believe in Anika. She is within you. Anika is you. Together you will inspire the world."

I now call my soul Anika; it is Anika who is having the human experience of Lauren here on earth during this lifetime. I have recognized my connection with spirit and welcomed my higher self into my life. Anika is unique and yet an integral part of God and All that Is. Anika is my SOULworks. In fact, the month I opened my SOULworks business was the same month my spirit guides had predicated Anika's arrival three year's prior - September 11, 2011.

Activating your SOULworks

I truly believe the entire message was always on the tablet. I just never took the time to look, was unwilling to see the truth or quickly jumped to a conclusion without truly looking at the situation in its entirety. This is especially common when we see a vision within our dreams that startles us awake. Once our earthly mind becomes alert, it will always try to include its two cents. To my earthly mind, the concept of my higher self had yet to even surface. It was a reality my ego was not willing to let in. However, my inner light strengthened along the way until it came to a point where I was forced to look at the bigger picture and see the entire vision for what it really was. The birth of my SOULworks.

Accounts of being reborn have surfaced around the world since the beginning of time. I have certainly not been the first. To be quite honest, I have always scoffed at these accounts. After all, what did it truly mean to be reborn? We were already born when we came to this earth. Mine was May 29, 1972 as my parents joyfully welcomed me into their world as a bouncing baby girl. My traditional birth in 1972 occurred when my higher self stepped aside to allow my spirit into the earthly body of Lauren. This was the start of my journey as Lauren while here on earth within this lifetime. I have had many more.

My rebirth occurred the day my earthly body stepped aside and welcomed my divine spirit into the journey. It is not that my divine spirit was never present. It is that I never had the presence to recognize the divine within.

Your Move:

- ❑ **Meet your soul.** In your mind, journey slightly above your head to your soul star. You will know you have reached the right place when you see a translucent light and feel a familiarity of home. In the centre of this star is a door with light radiating out from all around it. Bravely walk up to the door, open it up, and step inside. Greet the light being that resides within. Ask its name. Trust in the answer you receive. Once you have met your higher self, let its presence shine into your life.

- ❑ **Closely review repeating messages.** Do you experience reoccurring dreams, visions, and premonitions that continue to repeat, and repeat, and repeat, and repeat, and repeat? These are the messages you should pay close attention to. Chances are, you have misinterpreted their intended meaning. Reoccurring dreams are always for a reason. Your spirit guides take a lot of time and energy to try to get a message across to you. Please take the time to listen. If the message does not make any sense, request more information or zoom in closer and see what it is you may have missed.

❏ **Listen to insights.** You are involved in conversations on a daily basis. The mailman, the lady next door, your co-workers, your children, your spouse, your waitress, and even complete strangers all have something to say. Sometimes their messages are directed specifically towards you and hold a key to your divine path. Actively listen to these conversations. Even take the time to watch their expressions. I have witnessed the face of a complete stranger morph into that of a loved one without them even realizing. In this state, they have delivered a message of love straight to me without even skipping a beat in our conversation. Do not let your mind wander. Stay in the now and be present. To do so is to recognize and receive the presence of spirit.

❏ **Activate your rebirth.** In truth, you have already activated your rebirth by learning to expand you mind. However, once you have met your higher self and welcomed its wisdom and infinite presence into your life, move this part of you into the depths of your heart, placing your higher self further and further into the core of your very being. To do so, is to be reborn.

CHAPTER 18

Healing Energies

I cannot accurately pinpoint the day I truly started to feel healing energies pouring out of my hands. It was a gradual process that perhaps started with my mom, and continued to grow and blossom from that day forward. Just like a tiny seed planted within the garden of life, my healing abilities started as a small kernel of potential. Through experience and guidance, the seeds were planted, watered and cared for, and the energy began to grow. Like the progression of all evolution, the growth started from the heavens and slowly began to reach down towards earth, becoming stronger and more grounded along the way.

At first, I felt healing energy as a small but distinct tingling sensation emanating from the palms of my hands. This phenomenon usually occurred when I knew someone was suffering or while I was looking at someone in need. Whether a person's suffering stemmed from a health problem, emotional trauma, family ties or even work-related issues, the cause did not seem to matter. A person in need is a person in need. At some point along the way, when I felt or saw someone's hardship, my heart would open and my hands automatically began to tingle with energy.

I remember a particular incident while walking alone one day enjoying the sunshine and fresh air. Along my stroll, I came across a family. The father was in a wheel chair and appeared to have suffered a stroke. His family pushed him along the path in silence, their sadness deafening. As we crossed paths, I was overcome by the strongest urge to reach out and help. Echoing in my mind I heard the words "you should lay your hands on this man." I wish I could say I listened to this inner guidance, but like so many other times in my life, I just shook my head in disbelief.

Touching someone to provide comfort is actually a natural instinct we all possess. We all have the innate ability to show empathy and then act upon this intuitive desire to help someone. It is why a mother will instinctively reach out to comfort her child or why hugs can magically erase any troubles away. Although I had experienced empathy in the past, I was never so driven to reach out and touch a complete stranger. What would they think of me? What would I say? The idea seemed so ludicrous; did I really think I could help this man? What was I thinking?

Besides my earlier lack of confidence in healing, the issue I originally had was distinguishing between my thoughts and the guidance I receive from spirit. There is only a slight difference in the way spirit communicates with me and the way I silently talk to myself. Spirit speaks in the third person; I dialogue with myself in the first. Notice how I did not hear the words "I should lay my hands on this man." If I had been more knowledgeable and confident in myself at this point in my life, I would have recognized spirit was asking me to help this complete stranger. Had I been brave enough to reach out and touch him, the interaction would have proven miraculous for us both. Years later, I can confidently say spirit does not ask you to reach out and physically help someone for no reason. I also know that the laying on of hands has created many miracles, past and present. When you reach out to touch someone from the heart, a healing on some level will always occur. And here's a thought: Why wait for spirit to ask at all? Why not just reach out and send someone the healing energies of love?

There is one more difference between my self-talk and the words of wisdom provided by spirit. Spirit speaks in a calm and gentle manner and often brings thoughts that would never have crossed my mind. In fact, this red flag has become my spiritual healing 911 alert, my bat signal of sorts. Whenever I hear myself saying, "why in the world would I think that" or "what was I possibly thinking" while having a positive and caring thought about someone, I stop to truly ponder if spirit was communicating and then I respond. Despite my initial lack of confidence and my communication breakdowns, healing energies do emanate from my hands. Spirit does ask me to help those in need. More importantly, the further I strive to help, the stronger those healing energies have become.

For years, I have felt this healing energy and have grown to accept it as truly there and a part of who I am. I have also come to realize I can access this universal energy whenever and wherever appropriate. I now strive to utilize these gifts as often as possible, and honestly it feels wonderful.

I cannot accurately pinpoint the day I started to feel healing energies pouring out of my hands. But I can say, what originally started as a feeling, moved to a trusting, and finally actively using my God-given potential. When I finally left my inhibitions behind and began to utilize the healing force within, the energy in my hands moved from a small tingling sensation to radiating a spiritual force resembling a fire hydrant on full throttle. Furthermore, it was within this trust and determination, I successfully moved beyond just feeling the energy, to actually seeing this God-given universal light springing from my hands.

The first time I visually witnessed this energy was while studying spiritual healing abroad. Participants from all over the world gathered to learn how to conduct healing sessions, to better understand healing energy, and to fully trust in their abilities. I had travelled half way across the globe to learn from the best healers in the world, to learn their techniques, and to study their methods. What I discovered during this life changing experience was breathtaking. My spirit guides provided many visions, unlocked many mysteries, and provided various insights over the course of my studies. However, the message throughout the duration of the training was very clear: I was already intuitively using the methods being taught at the college. I had travelled miles to learn from the best healers in the world, only to discover I was already one of them. As I opened my eyes during the healing session startled by this realization, I looked down at my hands with tears streaming down my cheeks. I was glowing in golden light and radiating this golden energy from my palms, fingertips, third eye, and even my heart.

Years of trusting and blindly moving ahead on sheer faith alone had finally paid off. The old adage "seeing is believing" continues to dominate our world, but I promise you this is a huge misrepresentation of the actual process. Believing is seeing.

Activating your SOULworks

There are many historical paintings and biblical references illustrating radiant glow emanating from within. Halos and beams of light are depicted as an energetic force field encompassing individuals who have achieved spiritual enlightenment. We currently live in a society where these symbols of grace are reserved for great ones such as saints or divine leaders of the world who walked the earth before our time. This is our culture. This is what we have been taught to believe.

However, we all have the power to access the light within and radiate it out into the world. We all have the ability to glow from the inside out, heal the sick, and end our suffering. In fact, once you begin to notice the energy around and within you, you will also begin to notice the light vibrating around every living thing. If you look closer, you will even visually see many people within our society whose light is strong and vibrant.

My son was one of the first people to witness the light energy that radiates from my hands. It occurred out of the blue one day when he and I were working on a project together. We were both busy at work when all of a sudden, my son jumped back with a startled expression on his face, blinking wildly. I asked what was wrong and he cautiously indicated, "It was nothing. Never mind." Knowing full well he had definitely seen something out of his ordinary reality I pried a little further. "No really. Tell me what you saw." Living the life I lead, I was expecting him to confide he saw a spirit or perhaps an orb of light. However, his words hit way closer to home. My son explained how for a brief moment in time he saw a beam of light streaming out of my hands. He described it as a large, blinding light that he had never seen before. Ironically, this occurred before I had actually confided in seeing or feeling the divine light myself. Determined to speak my truth and make my son understand what he had witnessed was real, I excitedly responded, "That is because you did see a light. That is the healing energy I radiate. I have seen it too."

Visually you can actually see the connection people have with the spirit world and those who have activated the healing powers within. There is a glow around people who are no longer living in darkness and are growing their awareness of being one with the universe. People from all over the world are awakening to this reality and are being called to activate their God-given potential. I repeat: We are the ones we have been waiting for.

Your Move:

❑ **See the light.** Take a closer look at your surroundings. Watch the trees, animals, buildings, and people that are all around you. Notice the vibrational energy of light that surrounds all things. Watch as the light increases and decreases in size and shape depending on external and internal factors. Let your eyes relax and just observe. Notice how sad people have an auric field close to their bodies. See the large glow around someone who is happy and content. Make a point of watching an inspired speaker talk about their life's passions. Watch as their energy field expands and the light around them radiates to fill the room. Focus specifically on the shoulder and head area. Those who have a strong connection with spirit will emanate various colors of the rainbow. They will appear lighter than others and will literally just glow.

❑ **Be the light.** We have access to the light of the world and it would be a crying shame to continue living in darkness. Harness this light energy and direct it out into your world. Imagine a portal opening up between heaven and earth and direct this blessed energy to flow freely between the worlds. Visualize the light emanating from your hands. Feel the tingling or pulsating sensations. Sit within this energy and feel the warmth and comfort of its power. To help society transition, gracefully accept your divine connection to All that Is, inspire the world around you to truly begin to live, and set an example of enlightenment by letting your inner light shine.

❑ **Shine your light.** Learn to harness your energy healing powers and abilities. All it takes is imagination, determination, and intention. Set your intention to heal. Visualize within your mind someone or something in need. You do not need to know where the problems lie; you only need to hold the intention to help restore perfect balance. Pull the light down from heaven and surround your entire being. Push this energy towards the earth. You can make no mistakes when sending energy from a place of love. You are a holder of this light. Direct this energy to any area that is unbalanced within your world. This can be a physical body, emotional traumas, a physical place, situation or thing. Radiate this energy as brightly and as widely as possible. You are the light of the world.

❑ **Accept your light.** Strive to improve your life and increase your vibrational energy through good deeds. Take on activities that help the environment, share with those in need, honor our animal kingdom, and heal our world. After all, not all heroes wear capes. Heroes are everyday people like you and me who live from the heart. Never fear that you are coming from a place of ego. Anyone who has the compassion to help the world is always coming from the heart. It is okay to let yourself be big and powerful when you are striving to make the world a better place. The world needs your energy and enthusiasm. The world needs your light.

CHAPTER 19

Divine Acceptance

T his is the chapter I hesitate to include in my book. For to do so is to even further open myself to judgment and ridicule. However, I ask you to listen to my stories with an open mind. If you consider that our thoughts create our reality, then even if you hesitate to believe in my accounts, why would you not want to create a reality that is so blessed?

As I have mentioned before, angels and spirit guides do speak to me. They ask me to send healing energies out into the world and have been a critical part of activating my own SOULworks. I have learned how to work with the angels, asking for their divine assistance to heal the sick and bless the emotionally wounded. The archangels have always been incredibility receptive and join me in all healing sessions. However, the day my healing abilities really ramped up began when I actively became more involved in the process.

I have heard many schools of thought, but most insist humans need to step out of the way during a healing session. It is often recommended we become passive participants in the healing process and call upon the angels and/or God to do the job for us. I only partially agree with this theory. I believe our earthly minds do need to step aside so we can fully access the heavenly realms; however, our souls ARE the universal spirit. We can commune within all dimensions and have access to this energy source ourselves because we are contained within it. In fact, we are this energy force. So yes, we can step aside and let someone else do the job of healing. We can continue to call to the heavens for help or even choose to do nothing at all and remain victims of our own circumstances. Or, we can become an active participant in our existence and evolution. We are the ones here on earth capable of making a change to our own reality by utilizing our own free will. Right here. Right now. Our souls have the ability to heal and bless all we come into contact with, as long as our intentions are pure and from the heart. Once I reached this milestone realization in my own healing practice, I truly stepped into my divine light.

Instead of waiting for my divine team to pay me a visit (which of course they still do and I love to have their involvement), I also take the time to venture up towards the heavens and initiate my own development. While in the angelic realm, I have visions of wondrous beauty and am guided to utilize various healing techniques. I was also provided with a healing temple from which to channel the energies. Here I have access to administer energetic operations, crystal therapies, attunements, balancing and strengthening the chakra systems, and many other divinely inspired practices. In doing so, I have moved across the bridge into oneness.

It is within the acceptance of oneness I began to expand my visions and abilities. On one particular day, while visiting the realms of spirit I had a vision of a great white buffalo. Our spirits became one as she let me climb upon her back, taking in her great strength and endurance. She told me I too must be strong. This great white buffalo led me through a tunnel of colors into another dimension where all the animal spirit guides reside. The white buffalo told me to visit this place often and use its energies to help with healing. Since that day, I utilize the inner strength and endurance of the great white buffalo that is now a part of me. I also utilize the spiritual strength of other animal spirits such as the bear and birds. All these spirit guides are great healers and messengers of God that have become a part of who I am.

Another vision involved the meaning and power behind the medicine wheels. These purposefully created monuments symbolize how we are all interconnected: people, animals, earth, the universe, and creator. At the very centre of the wheel is where your spirit stands and it is within this centre you find God; not out in the universe, but centred and concentrated within you. It is healing to acknowledge this oneness of interconnectivity. The stones point to astronomy and the directions of time, but they are also grounded and point to the centre within us all. Since that day, the symbol of a medicine wheel radiates from my hands, heart, and third eye. It has also become a part of who I am. The symbol is used to remind people of our oneness with the universe.

On another occasion, I had a vision of Yeshua hanging on the cross. However, it was not during the time of the crucifixion. Instead he was still hanging on the cross in spirit, but within the present time. I was there helping to take him down. I thanked my dear friend for holding the space for society for so long. I told him I was ready to step into my power, to help others find theirs, and to follow in his example. We embraced and then journeyed back to my homeland. I utilize the knowledge of this avatar and follow his lead to manifest miracles. He is a part of me, and I a part of him. Similarly, I have also embraced the spiritual energy of other healers such as Moses, Buddha, and the archangels.

Still on another occasion, I had a vision where I journeyed to sit in the light of God. This time spirit laid hands on me and surrounded me with golden sparkling energy. Spirit explained I could use this energy to instantly manifest miracles. I then flew around to all family and friends blessing each and every one of them. From there, I flew around the world blessing others in need and offering healing energies abundantly.

Once a person reaches a point along their spiritual path where you can acknowledge and accept your oneness to the universe, you are able to access and utilize the strength and abilities of any other spirit force within the realms. For to do so, is to simply access and accept the force that already resides within you. These fragments within you existed as a whole before we pulled apart and became individuals living in darkness.

To explain this further, we are all energy. On a soul level, our energy is part of a greater source of All that Is. Within this source resides the energetic spirits of everything that has ever been or will ever be. This includes humans, animals, nature, our earth, our galaxy, and the spirit world from beyond. Energetically we all exist as one.

As your awareness increases, your own energy source can expand to include the energies and strengths of other spirits. This is not to say you are the only one who can access this energy, for it is infinite and omnipresent. Anyone has the potential to expand consciousness and tap into the energy fields of other great spirits such as the ascended masters who walked the earth before our time, the energetic greatness of the animal kingdom, angelic realm, Mother Earth, and the list goes on. There really is no limit to the energy you can combine and harness from this wondrous source of All that Is. Your abilities will expand as you begin to accept this divine greatness within you.

Sometimes your energetic fields are combined with a spiritual energy of a specific angel or ascended master because you have made the request personally. Other times, like my vision of the white buffalo, the spirit will make its presence known to you and start working with you along your journey. As you work together, your energetic field becomes one and your abilities while here on earth strengthen, as you begin to take on the characteristics of this spirit. For a white buffalo, this includes the strength to move forward and the unwavering faith of miracles. Both characteristics I certainly needed to add to my repertoire at the time of the vision.

I also find people are drawn to certain spiritual guides relating to their own personal interests and soul path. For example, I work with the healers of the world: Yeshua, Moses, Archangel Raphael, and so on. As we all come from the same source energy, we are all one. All of these spiritual beings have made themselves known to me and all are present during my healing sessions. Our energies are combined and we heal as one.

Are you still with me? Good, because we are going to push this concept one step further. As I have already mentioned, we are all souls having a human experience here on earth. Understand everyone's soul is capable of tapping into divine energy, and with this powerful force, have the ability to light up our world. Furthermore, each soul has the power to heal and create our realities. And here is the great part: we do not even have to check out of this world in physical form to access our higher self and actively return to the heavenly realms, despite what our society has believed and preached for centuries. We can actually travel to this dimension at any time to access the wisdom of the ages, to channel the healing energies of the divine, to visit with our loved ones, heal our wounds, and to join our higher self together with the spirits of the ascended masters before us. Ascension is when humans give permission to reunite with their divine wholeness while staying on earth in physical body. The doorway to this wonderful existence is found within our heart. I choose to travel and live within this spirit world. I choose to stand in my divine light every day. What do you choose?

Activating your SOULworks

Start moving your awareness within. It is here that all the answers lie. A good starting place is within the chakras. These energy centres run vertically up your body and connect you vibrationally to the universal power. These energy centres guide our development here on earth and correlate to our physical, emotional, and spiritual growth. You can strengthen the connection between each energy centre and the energy of the universe simply by drawing a path within your mind for the energy to flow.

The human body has seven primary chakras that are most critical for healing and strengthening your awareness while here on earth. The chakras start at the base of the pelvis, move up to the crown of your head, and follow the colors of the rainbow. There are more chakras within your body, above and below. However, balancing the primary energy centres is a great starting point. It is within these energy centres that we have the ability to restore harmony to the body, mind, and soul.

Start at your Base/Root Chakra. Visualize this energy centre as vibrant red. This chakra is your survival and security centre. This governs your home life, financial abundance, connection to earth, and animal instinct. Balancing the Root Chakra helps increase your overall health and energy. It also helps with any body parts located below the spinal column. Send the energy from the base chakra within you, up to Source, and back down towards you in a perfect circular motion. Visualize the connection as strong and vibrant, ever flowing and ever abundant.

Next, move to the Sacral Chakra located in the lower abdomen. This chakra is your zone for creativity, relationships, procreation, joy, and pleasure. Balancing this chakra will help balance all these aspects in your life, and also help with any body parts within this region. Visualize this chakra as a powerful and vibrant orange. Send the energy from the Sacral Chakra within you, up to Source, and back down towards you in a perfect circular motion. Visualize the connection as strong and vibrant, ever flowing and ever abundant.

Move your way up to the Solar Plexus located in the area just above the navel. This is your power centre and is as bright and golden as the sun. Also governed in this area are aspects of your self-confidence, self-esteem, and manifestations. Balancing this chakra will help you stand in your divine light and actively create your life. On a physical perspective, balancing this chakra will help with the stomach, liver, gall bladder, and other organs within this area. Visualize this chakra as a powerful and vibrant yellow. Send the energy from the Solar Plexus within you, up to Source, and back down towards you in a perfect circular motion. Visualize the connection as strong and vibrant, ever flowing and ever abundant.

Next, we travel to the Heart Chakra located in the centre of the chest. This area focuses on love, compassion, hope, and forgiveness. Balancing this chakra also helps with the heart, circulatory system, lungs, ribs, hands, and diaphragm. Visualize this chakra as a powerful and vibrant green. Send the energy from the Heart Chakra within you, up to Source, and back down towards you in a perfect circular motion. Visualize the connection as strong and vibrant, ever flowing and ever abundant.

Moving further towards the heavens we enter your throat area. The Throat Chakra governs your expression, communication, and inner voice. It is here where you learn to speak your truth. Balancing this chakra will help with these aspects of your life, as well as any physical problems with your throat, teeth, jaw, and neck. Visualize this chakra as a powerful and vibrant robins' egg blue. Send the energy from the Throat Chakra within you, up to Source, and back down towards you in a perfect circular motion. Visualize the connection as strong and vibrant, ever flowing and ever abundant.

Place your focus on your Third Eye Chakra. This is located in the centre of your forehead and is your perception centre. It is here you expand your psychic consciousness, wisdom, and intuitive ability to visualize and access the power of the mind. Balancing this chakra also helps with the neurological system, eyes, ears, and nose. Visualize this chakra as a powerful and vibrant indigo. Send the energy from the Third Eye Chakra within you, up to Source, and back down towards you in a perfect circular motion. Visualize the connection as strong and vibrant, ever flowing and ever abundant.

Next, work on your Crown Chakra located at the top of your head. This is your spiritual centre where you can further develop your psychic abilities, attain enlightenment, and embrace unity. Balancing this chakra system also helps with the central nervous system, the muscular system, and the skin. Visualize this chakra as a powerful and vibrant purple. Send the energy from the Crown Chakra within you, up to Source, and back down towards you in a perfect circular motion. Visualize the connection as strong and vibrant, ever flowing and ever abundant.

Lastly focus on your Soul Star located above your head. This is your connection to your soul and is reflected in a white glowing light. Visualize a figure eight that moves from this Soul Star, up to Source, back down to your Soul Star, and then follow this through with a downward motion to your Heart Chakra and then back up to your Soul Star. This energy flow strengthens our infinite connection from our body, to our soul, and to God. Visualize the connection as strong and vibrant, ever flowing and ever abundant.

This is one method I recommend you use on a regular basis to bring awareness to your energy centres and connection to the divine. It can also be utilized during healing sessions for others. Energetically strengthening this connection will help bring clarity to your visions, intuition, and communications with spirit.

Your Move:

❑ **Develop a spiritual practice.** If you have not already done so, take at least ten minutes everyday to travel into the spiritual realms and sit in the divine light of All that Is. Use your imagination to allow yourself to leave your body and expand your mind. Move closer to Source energy and your divine connection. Try different experiences and let yourself stop at various locations along the way. You are always safe and accompanied by your spirit guides. Never fear the unknown. Just surrender yourself to the light and let your soul take you on a journey.

❑ **Dance.** The connection you have with the spirit world is a magical dance between our worlds. The more you connect, the closer your dimensions become and the more in tune you will be with your spiritual self. Balancing your chakras is a wonderful way to connect this energy source, and I invite you to practice this art daily. However, if you really want to step it up, dance with the spirit world. That's right. Leave all your inhibitions behind and just dance. Think about your departed loved ones or spirit guides; invite them to join you in a dance. Feel their closeness. Gracefully glide through this thing we call life to the beat of your souls. Give your spirit permission to dance.

❑ **Meet your power animals.** Hold the intention of meeting your power animal. Journey into the animal kingdom by moving through a tunnel of rainbow colors. Once you enter this dimension stop and take a minute to observe. What do you see? If you have a vision of an animal or become one with their spirit, do not dismiss this as ridiculous. Instead, learn about the animal and what their power symbolizes. One of the first power animals I ever saw was a bear. I actually used to fear bears. However, as my awareness increased I realized a bear is symbolic of a healer (and ironically, I used to fear my healing abilities). What are your power animals? What paths are you destined to venture down?

❑ **Heed guidance from your visions.** Visions are intended to provide you with guidance, messages, ideas or processes you can utilize to develop as a soul. When you start to journey into the spiritual realms, your visions are going to increase. Pay attention to the signs and information you receive. Become an active participant in your spiritual growth by venturing into these realms. Actively take the information you receive while on your journey. Make changes in your life accordingly so you may truly shine. To do so is wonderfully enlightening.

CHAPTER 20

Take My Hand

B ecoming more attuned to spirit takes time and practice. There are many different ways to become one with spirit and move between the spiritual dimensions. I will provide an overview of the method I often utilize. This does not mean it is the only way or the best way. Everyone is unique and everyone will have their own special way to connect and move between the realms. There is also no special order that needs to be completed. I am often asked to explain the exact steps I use: "Do you take a breath, move up into spirit and then send healing or do you move up into spirit, send healing, and then take a breath?" Really it does not matter. Do what feels natural. Give your own mind the creative freedom to develop a process that is right for you.

While connected to spirit, do not be afraid to think while you are in this deep attunement. Oftentimes, we are taught to stop our mind from thinking and bring our awareness back to total blankness. That is not necessarily good advice. Perhaps you receive your intuitive information through claircognition, which is a clear knowing. Information drops into my mind all the time. If I do not take the time to process the visions I am receiving, then I am missing out on the messages all together.

Let's begin this guided healing journey. Start your journey by imagining you are walking outside. Enjoy the sounds of the birds, the warmth from the sun, and the comfort from the energy that is all around you. Give thanks to Mother Earth for providing this wonderful sanctuary. Notice the cloud that has slowly manifested near your feet. Move forward and gracefully step onto the cloud. Once on the cloud, your spirit guides greet you with open arms. Your spirit guides are always by your side and present on every journey. One of your spirit guides has extended a hand out towards you. Take their hand and follow their lead. Peacefully sit back and enjoy the ride as the cloud begins to ascend into heaven. There are many levels to this divine kingdom and many spiritual beings along the way. Watch for the level with the rainbow over the golden door. This will be your first stop for the day. Smoothly glide from your resting place upon the cloud and move towards the door. Feel the magical bliss of the rainbow as you walk straight through this sacred energy and through the door. What do you see? Let your mind take you where it wants to go. Is there someone waiting for you? What do they have to say? Ask them a question regarding your soul path and trust in the answer you receive. Take as much time as you want here. Experience the landscape. Let the nearby waterfall cleanse your very being and reach down into the depths of your soul. Sit in this power and soak up the energy and the rays of light. Let this divine light grow within you until your soul expands out to every corner of the heavens. When you are ready to leave this space, give thanks and carry on with your journey.

Watch for the cloud. It will be right there by your feet again. Step onto the cloud with grace and confidence as you ascend further into the heavens. Watch for the emerald colored door. This is your next stop for today. Again, walk through the rainbow and into the room. Look all around you and bask in the light of your healing temple. What do you see? Take in the splendor of the architectural designs held within this sacred space. View the columns of stone and the open roof that extends far into the universe. Observe the power in this room. Walk over to the middle of the room towards the rainbow alter. Ask the universe where healing energies are required today. Watch or listen for the answer. Trust in the response and start to visualize the person, place or thing you are to help.

Watch as the floor of your healing temple begins to slide open. Observe as a portal begins to form and the healing energy begins to flow towards your target. Visualize the energy as it flows from the healing temple and surrounds those in need. Zoom closer into the situation. What do you see? Are there any places of darkness? Are there areas you are attracted to? Concentrate your efforts on these areas. Send light toward the areas in need. Move the energy like you are conducting an orchestra. Rebalance the chakra energy systems of the body and restore order to all areas. Trust in your ability to do so. Start narrowing the gap between the person receiving the healing and your healing temple. Move the energies until they are all right in front of you. Place your hands on the person, bless them, and watch as the energy pours from your hands into their body. Remove dark energies by using your imagination. Restore balance and order. Send love.

Continue to use your creativity to help heal. Feel free to use the crystals that are sitting by your side to help increase your intentions and power. Use some of the sacred water to purify the body, mind, and soul. Send butterflies of light to help with the transformation. Move the person right through the colors of the rainbow. Place a symbolic medicine wheel on top of the area in need. Trust in the miracles that are unfolding. Find pride in what you are doing. Give thanks to yourself for striving to make a difference. Give thanks to God.

Slowly begin to distance your target from the healing temple. Ask your guides and angels to continue sending healing energies towards the person, place or thing. Trust in the process and divine order of things. Notice as the cloud has appeared under your feet. This time, move in any direction you desire. Select a new door, the one with the rainbow radiating above. Open the door and look inside. Trust in what you see. Let your higher self and angelic team sweep you away on your journey. You are here to learn. Watch the visions that unfold before you. Listen for the wisdom that is provided. Heed the advice. Move further into the light and across the rainbow bridge. Take a leap of faith.

When you feel your journey is complete for the day, gracefully take the hand of your spirit guide and step back onto the cloud. Watch as the cloud begins to descend back down to our present realm. Believe in the visions you have seen. Give thanks for the experience.

Once you have mastered this level, take someone else on your travels. I used to only travel on these journeys alone, partially because I was nervous to explain my visual realities to others, and partially because I was just learning. I would view the areas that needed to be worked on and then silently send healing energies. The first time I was guided to bring someone else along on the journey with me, I was working on a friend from a distance. Over the phone, I asked her to take my hand and together we ascended into heaven on a cloud. I walked her through the various levels from visiting the healing temple, to viewing past lives, to visiting her future endeavors. After we were finished the journey, we discussed the experience and shared our encounters. It was so amazing and eye-opening to hear how vivid the journey had been for my friend. How she had witnessed the areas I was describing before I even started to describe them. My friend could feel the heat and tingling on the body parts just seconds before I started to explain where I was working. The details were astounding and we both found the journey to be very healing. Since that day, I have continued to use this method in my healings. My previous clients always had a positive experience, but never so profound as the day I started to include them along my travels to the spirit world. Take my hand.

Your Move:

❑ **Be active.** My healing temple manifested during a time I was struggling with my studies on becoming a passive participant to healing. Within this space I am able to be myself, to add my own flair and unique energy to a healing. You can utilize a similar space such as a healing temple or create your own place of power. However, know that when you are utilizing your imagination to move into the spirit world, your earthly body has in fact stepped aside and you are manifesting a healing. Within this space, there is no limit to what you can heal. The sky is the limit.

❑ **Involve others.** Once you have utilized this technique, try taking someone else on this guided healing journey. Trust in your ability to escort them along a path of healing. Give it a try and then be sure to compare notes. You will be surprised how visual and accurate the experience was for both of you. There are three methods to sending healing towards someone within a guided journey:

    ❍ Hands on – To conduct hands on healing with someone, you as the healer, place your hands on the client. This can simply be to hold hands or to place your hands on their shoulders. Please ask their permission before proceeding. With their permission, take them along on a guided healing journey.

○ Distance – Distance healing is conducted by being in the same room as the person, but not actually having physical contact. To start the healing process, simply hold the intention to help your client for their highest good, and establish eye contact to get the energy flowing.

○ Absent – Absent healing occurs when you are not in close proximity to the person to whom you are channelling energy. There is no limit to the distance spanning between you. All you need to do is set your intention to send healing energies. You may find it effective to look at a photo of the person or envision them in your mind's eye. Furthermore, because in this example we are taking the person on a guided healing journey, you can access a web cam or telephone to help implement the expedition.

❑ **Visit your soulful past.** Your entire being is made up of lifetimes of experiences, not all of which are from here on earth. Our universe is infinite and the life of your soul is the same. Expand your mind into who you are and where you come from. It is this compilation of lives, life lessons, trials, and tribulations that make you who you are. Honor your uniqueness. Enter the spirit world for the purpose of retrieving information from your past lives that are not of this world. This can be information you need to help make sense of a current situation, information that will help move you forward along your journey, or information on past lives that may be holding you back and making you scared to make life changes. Delve into this timeline and introduce yourself to the whole you.

❑ **Open doors.** Let your cloud take you wherever it wants to go. Open new doors and try new experiences. You never know what magical moment awaits you. On some levels, you will be able to clearly see and interact with your departed loved ones. On others, you will be introduced to the fairy world. Other levels house your angelic team and are also used for ceremonies in your honor. Open the door and step in.

CHAPTER 21

Infinite Power

The amount of energy you can channel towards a person, place or thing is infinite and only limited by your mind. As I mentioned earlier, there is no one method or right way to access this source energy within your mind. All methods work and are unique to your very being. I utilize the cloud technique a lot because as soon as I step on the cloud, my mind shifts and I enter my intuitive zone. This is a trained response I utilize for two purposes: to quickly reach this level of attunement, and then also to return to my earthly body in a disciplined manor. However, once I am in the zone, I have also utilized many different methods and techniques to send energy. This chapter will give a brief overview of a few of my favorites.

Exercise:

I often utilize the energy force created through exercise to propel energy towards a person in need. As I walk or bike, I will envision I am generating and directing healing energy, watching the area become clean and full of light. One of the first times I was guided to use this technique was while I was actually trying to get up the motivation to exercise. I always found myself coming up with excuses not to actively move my body on a daily basis. Not because it did not feel great, but because I preferred to spend any of my spare time on my own SOULworks, sending healing energies to those in need. One day, I was inspired to combine the two practices and the results were truly amazing. I was so energized during the workout, that I pushed beyond my usual steady pace. I was literally like a seasoned athlete running a marathon. Well, a walker on a mini marathon anyway.

During the process, I also found the energy I generated even more intense and my ability to visually see my client from a distance significantly intensified. I could literally zoom into their physical body and see what areas needed work, viewing areas with accurate detail and precision. I could also visually observe when the healing was complete and the energies rebalanced.

Please understand that you do not need to know where the energy is going for a healing to occur. Healing energy always goes where it is needed and it never fails. However, being able to see the areas where a healing is taking place is helpful to confirm and validate the experience. No matter how many times I have successfully sent healing energy, I am always humbled by the results. It is truly amazing to hear validation of the dis-ease that was present within the exact area of the body I was focusing my intentions on, as well as confirmation on the areas later becoming balanced and successfully healed.

⸺⸻◆⸻⸺

Singing:

I have already spoken to the healing benefits sound has to the body, mind, and soul. I utilize sound vibrations to help increase the strength and intentions of my energy healing sessions. Sound can literally heal the sick. Its vibrational frequencies carry with it a healing energy that speaks to us on a soul level. I use this knowledge and the power of song to better my health and the health of others.

Although I have yet to conjure up the confidence to sing to a client, I do utilize this method when sending healing energies, while in the safety and privacy of my own home. I select a song that speaks to me about the person in need, and then sing with all my heart and soul. While harmonizing with the angels, I send this energetic force towards the person being healed, watching it cleanse their very being and help them along their journey.

The first time I sang a song with the intention of healing was for a terminally ill friend. The song of choice was nothing I would normally have used, but the words spoke volumes and just started to flow. Although my friend passed on, please remember that a healing will always occur on some level, it may just not be clear to our earthly vision. The depths of our souls are vast and infinite. I also know, in some way the song made a difference to my friend and helped with his transition. In fact, I hear from his spirit every time that the song plays on the radio to this very day.

Angelic Wings:

We are all spiritual beings larger than life. We are all connected to everything that ever was and ever will be. We are all divine. Therefore, it should be no surprise that we can achieve an angelic level just as our counterparts in the heavens. The first time I started to feel my energetic wings was very early on in my SOULworks. I did not have a frame of reference to compare my experience, but nevertheless, one day while sending energy to someone in need, I felt my wings energetically unfold from behind me and embraced the person with all my greatness. I could literally feel as the wings expanded and I stood in my power.

Think I am crazy? Well I sure did! I could not wrap my head around why I (a mere human and not always a good one at that) would have the wings of an angel. It must have been my imagination, right? And once again, who the hell did I think I was? However, despite my self-criticisms, the experience was very vivid and very real. It was during this experience that my abilities as a healer also increased. Once again, I felt the surge of energy move from me to the person in need and the healing powers significantly amplified.

This experience also triggered a memory, the memory of my mom recovering from her cardiac arrest so many years ago. I recalled the morning my dad had phoned to confirm the events that had transpired the night before. After receiving his call, I quickly acknowledged the accuracy of my visions and then started the 100km trek to the hospital. (Well actually, it was more of a "holy shit" moment and then a panicked urge to be near my mom). Before I arrived, I took the time to stop at a gift shop. I was looking for just the right way to express to my mom what had transpired during the night, the visions I had, and the healing energies I channelled towards her. My sights narrowed in on a book called *Wings of Silver*. I did not even open the book to see what was inside. It was the title that caught my eye and prompted me to purchase this perfect and simple, silver colored book.

As I neared the hospital, I was guided by spirit to include a message within the book. Although I was reluctant to inscribe the message I heard, I moved forward anyway with sheer faith. In remembering this memory years later, I could not actually recall the message I had included within. However, I knew it would hold wisdoms related to the experience I had just had with the angelic wings. Not so coincidental at all, I also found other people describing similar experiences while discovering their true identity within themselves. This knowledge and confirmation brought much comfort, for perhaps I was crazy, but at least I was not alone.

Years later, I mustered up the courage during a phone conversation to ask my mom about the book and the inscription within. Tears streamed down my face, as my mom read the simple but profound words I had written so many years ago in my gift to her, *Wings of Silver.*

> *To my mom,*
> *With her very own wings of silver.*
> *Love Lauren*

When I hung up the phone, my mind flashed back to the day I had written those touching words. At the time, there was a power struggle going on between what I believed to be true, and what I was being guided to write. I was clearly receiving guidance to write the words as I had eventually transcribed. However, my earthly mind was not okay with the message. It made no sense to me at the time. Yes, an angel had visited me that magical night. This being of light helped me see the power within, to send my mom love, and to channel healing energies. However, to state my mom had her own wings of silver was incomprehensible to me at the time. I argued with my guides, saying it made no sense. To that, I heard their calm and soothing reply, "Even so, please write the words, my child. In due time, you will understand."

That time has finally come. Those words written nearly twenty years ago, returned into my conscious awareness on the day I needed them most; the day I felt my energetic wings and my true divine self. And do you know what? Turns out I am not crazy. My mom has had me tested.

Activating your SOULworks

As you become more and more aware of the spirit world, your true self will begin to surface. Trust in the information you receive. There was a time in my life when I would never have believed who I am as a soul and what I have come to earth to accomplish. As I developed my knowledge base and experiences, I reached a point when I understood my SOULworks, but was still afraid to speak my truths to society. It took many years to decipher the messages and missed signals to truly understand and fear no more. It is at this point, that I finally conquered my fears of the unknown, learned to speak my truth, and started to share my experiences.

What I have also learned to understand is that if someone is not ready to hear these messages, they will skip over them, dismiss them as fiction or completely not even hear the message at all. We only see what we want to see or hear what we want to hear. Anything out of society's comfort zone or knowledge base is dismissed. And that is okay. Perhaps it is not a part of that person's soul path to discover their inner truth at that moment in time. However, there will come a day when each and every person on earth will experience their inner spirit starting to shine. And it is during these moments of enlightenment, that every single individual will take a second look at the road map of his or her soul. Everyone will begin to hear the messages of spirit and accept their true divinity; everyone, including you.

Your Move:

- ❑ **Step it up.** Exercise has always provided people with a strong connection to the divine. The term "runners high" is not a coincidence. Exercising your body literally increases your vibration, making it easier to connect to your higher

159

self. Take the time to exercise on a daily basis, regardless of the activity. However, instead of letting yourself mindlessly wander, hold the intention to send this increased vibration towards something in need. Push yourself further than you have ever gone and notice how much energy you can generate. Send this energy out into the world.

❑ **Sing.** The next time you or someone around you is feeling ill, sing to them with the intention of sending healing energy towards the inflicted area. Hold the intention that the sound vibrations are rebalancing all health problems, and rebooting their physical systems with grace and ease. Sickness is no more than a person's energy skipping to the beat of their soul. Find the scratch and apply soothing sounds generously.

❑ **Find your wings.** You are a divine being of the light. Your soul has lived through so many experiences that your earthly mind may find hard to comprehend. However, I encourage you to open your mind and look at the areas in life to which you have always been drawn. Do you have a fascination with the stars? Do you believe in fairies? Have you had angelic encounters? Can you communicate with the animal kingdom? Trust these experiences are providing a mere glimpse into the greatness you truly are. It is time to start finding your wings and opening your heart, so that together, we may spread our wings and fly.

❑ **Do a double take.** I have no doubt there have been many times in your life when you have read a book, heard someone's wisdom or experienced an event that you dismissed at the time as false or impossible. I know this to be true because I have done the same. I invite you to look again. Were there insights within the experience that you dismissed simply because they did not fall within your current state of awareness? If so, take another look. Read that book again. Retrace the steps of your past. Watch for the signs, and start to map together the workings of your soul. And by the way, do not ever, not even for one minute, feel bad about not awakening to this reality sooner. You are exactly where you are intended to be.

❑ **Amplify your light.** The impact of many is always far greater than one. Take your light and healing intentions out into the world. Actively look for a group of people who are interested in conducting the same work, at the same time all over the world. To do so is like combining battery packs to an already powerful source. The healing energy will grow exponentially. This has been proven through the power of prayer chains, large meditation groups, healing circles, and the like. Add your light to this ever-growing force of lightworkers.

Chapter 22

Disbelief

Over the years, I have suffered from more disbelief and confusion about my own personal experiences, with both spirit and my healing abilities, than reasonably imaginable. Nobody has doubted my abilities more than myself. It is for this very reason I will always completely understand why others question my claims. If it has taken me years to overcome my fears and reach a place in my life when I can confidently speak my truth, how can I ever expect others to understand only on hearsay?

Many have questioned the validity of my statements and the source of my information. Some question whether the events ever happened. Others ponder my mental health. A few have even suggested I work with Satan. I have had bible verses quoted, doubts expressed, and judgments made. But no matter how cruel or harsh their words may seem, I assure you their criticisms are never any more hurtful than what I have already said to myself. They have never provided an argument I have not already considered. Nobody has questioned the validity of why spirit would be working through me to heal, more than I have questioned myself.

Uncertainty and disbelief are a natural human response. People fear the unknown. We have been raised in a society with very limited spiritual knowledge. Many of our current religious systems are not inclusive of all that is contained in our universe, and countless truths are not discussed. Thankfully, there are still cultures around the world that have continued to practice spiritual growth, enlightenment, healing energy work, channelling of messages, and divinely inspired prophecies since the beginning of time. These practices are not evil, they are divinely inspired blessings that are clearly referenced in the Bible:

> *Now there are varieties of gifts, but the same Spirit; and there are varieties of service, but the same Lord; and there are varieties of activities, but it is the same God who empowers them all in everyone. To each is given the manifestation of the Spirit for the common good. For to one is given through the Spirit the utterance of wisdom, and to another the utterance of knowledge, to another faith, to another gifts of healing, to another the working of miracles, to another prophecy, to another the ability to distinguish between spirits, to another various kinds of tongues, to another the interpretation of tongues. All these are empowered by one and the same Spirit, who apportions to each one individually as he wills. (1 Corinthians 12:4-11 ESV)*

I find it both intriguing and sad how so many people believe in the miracles, healings, and teachings of the Bible, and yet disbelieve God would continue to touch our world and work through the common man. It breaks my heart to see how many people accept angels in biblical times, and yet dispel their presence in our everyday lives. Biblical times are nothing more than the ordinary, daily lives of the souls who walked the earth before us. To disbelieve the existence of angels, miracles, and healings conducted by everyday people within today's society, is to deny the power of spirit completely. After all, why would God be so connected and active in the lives of those who preceded us, and then be so absent in ours? The truth is, we are the ones who have removed ourselves from the divine connection with spirit. We are the ones who are no longer actively accepting spirit into our lives and believing in our God-given potential. We are the ones who have slowly changed over time. We are the ones who must open our eyes and see this truth.

Our world is within a transformational state. Like so many others, I believe many old souls have come to earth at this time to awaken our sleeping society and reclaim our gifts, intuition, loving purpose, and heavenly life. Ordinary people from every walk of life are becoming enlightened here on earth, just as a handful of others have achieved in the past. Similarly, just as in biblical times when healings and communication with spirit occurred, there are many miracles and many people around the globe who are seeing and channelling this light energy, with even more to come. There will also be many celebrations and many confirmations that God is facilitating miracles through every day people and changing the course of our history. We, as a society, are beginning to honor our truth as a divine part of spirit. This universal energy will sustain us all and we will shift consciousness to a new awakening. It is the dawn of the Golden Age.

I am confident and inspired by the much-needed changes occurring in our world and the truths finally being spoken. There are so many people around the globe having similar experiences to mine. Miraculous healings are occurring, people are actively speaking and communicating with spirit, brave souls are leaving their fears behind, and we, as a society, are moving forward to actively reclaim the power within.

No matter how scared I may be or how many doubters cross my path, I will continue to stand tall, speak my truth, and channel healing energies to those in need; for I am a healer, and a divine part of God. This is my purpose and the purpose of so many just like me. This growing, powerful, forward movement of change will bless our world, bringing heaven unto earth and peace unto mankind. Healing can occur one soul at a time, one prayer at a time, and one love at a time. We can affect change and the future of our world through our loving intentions. And change it, we will. Thanks be to God.

Activating your SOULworks

Whether you are a doubter or a believer, the important part is to open your mind to new ideas. There will never be a time when we have learned all there is to learn. Our world continues to evolve as our minds expand. Because our thoughts create our reality, there is no limit to what our future can bring. The stories I have included in this book are my realities as they exist today. I can honestly say with all my heart, that my life is truly miraculous. How is yours?

Your Move:

❑ **Notice the changes.** Books, songs, movies, television shows, clothing, games, as well as many other components in life, are beginning to increase in spiritual content and discuss topics that have been hushed for years. Welcome these much-needed changes into your life. Think back to movies you watched fifteen years ago that spoke of future technologies. Remember when you laughed at the ideas presented? Look at how far our society and technology has come. Spiritual awareness is the very same. Slowly but surely more information and ideas are being presented. Do not dismiss them as science fiction. Embrace the reality that your reality may be larger than first believed. Notice the changes happening as your awareness increases, and the veil between the dimensions slowly starts to disappear.

❏ **Start fresh.** I call a do over! Take all of your disbeliefs and throw them out the window. Challenge yourself to take a second look at anything you have ever doubted or believed as truths. Find your new truths by reviewing your old ideas and judgments. Dare to move into the unknown. Expand your horizons. Learn from your experiences. Continue to question your reality. Believe. As the world continues to transition, steadily and confidently breathe through the changes with love, not fear. Like a mother giving birth to a newborn child, so too will our society birth a new world. The darkness will lift and will most certainly be replaced with heaven on earth. Blessed be.

❏ **Embrace transformation.** Everything worth doing in life takes commitment, dedication, hard work, and time. It is this very reason why so many have struggled to reach enlightenment before our time. But you are well on your way and you will succeed. In fact, things are going to start falling into place very quickly, and your destiny will begin to take shape. You are a change maker. It is why you have felt restless in the past, and it is why you will be so successful in the future. As your mental tug of war continues to rise, be sure to stand your ground and continue to fight for what you believe in. Yes, you will be able to heal and help others, but you will do more than that. You will be a leader, providing hope, inspiration, and direction to many. Do not question whether you are making an impact. Just believe and know that you are.

❏ **Expand your horizons.** You already contain all the wisdom and knowledge that is needed within. However, there are many courses, books, and tools out there to help inspire your awareness. They are all wonderful resources. Follow your heart and move into your areas of interest. Get rid of your doubts and enjoy the now. Do not dwell on the outcome and future of your SOULworks. Trust you are growing, and in the meantime, continue to embrace life and raise your vibration.

CHAPTER 23

The Healing Journey Continues

I have spent a lot of time contemplating my life purpose. I was looking for a clear definition, a schedule of events, and explicit instructions on how I could best utilize my gifts to be of service to the world. My conclusions are not really what I had expected. My direction is still very vague, wide open, and full of opportunities that I have yet to even discover as part of my life's story.

I think that is because our life purpose is not intended to be so specific that we leave no room for growth and development. In looking at life from outside the box, it is not so important how we choose to have an adventure, so long as we strive to have one. It does not matter so much if we clearly see our path, so long as we start trusting and moving towards it. And it is certainly not important to define an exact plan of action for our life's story, so long as we learn to trust in the divine and leave room for the element of surprise and wonderment.

Be true to yourself and start living with purpose. Bring more joy into your world and to those around you. Take the time to celebrate life, share your gratitude, and watch for the beauty that is all around you. It is within these small but graceful actions that you manifest an inspired life and actively define who you are.

SOULworks is a lifetime of learning. The journey continues as I work to believe in my divine self and activate my potential within. To this day, I still cannot honestly say I successfully live day-to-day in my true power. I am, however, getting closer. It has taken a lot of personal experiences, soul searching, and support to come out of this spiritual closet; to defy the realities this world has asked me to believe as truths, and turn them upside down; and instead, to believe in myself, my experiences, and what I know to be true.

Angels and spirit guides are a huge part of my life. They have helped activate the healer within and continually provide the guidance and confidence I need to send love, light, and healing energies into the world; to pass on messages from the other side; and to stand up for what I believe in. I have grown to accept and honor this part of who I am. I have learned to proudly and firmly state my Declaration of Dependence to the world and to myself:

> *I, Lauren Heistad, am a healer and have had lifetimes of experiences to back this up. I am an inspiration to those in need and a teacher to others who aspire to do the same. I share the gift of healing wherever I go, and teach the art of creating miracles where my dear friend Jesus left off.*
>
> *I do not work independently. My declaration is dependant on God and the divine spark within us all to manifest change in this world. I work with the angels of God to heal the sick, create abundance, change lives, and bring balance to our dimension. I AM an essential component of the divine. I am here to help heal, change, and enlighten the world.* **This is who I am. This is my SOULworks.**

Activating your SOULworks

I have presented a lot of concepts, examples, and realities within the contents of this book. These are my truths. You need not accept them as I have presented. However, I do hope you will consider the possibilities. Learn from my experiences. Strive to improve your world and all those around you. Believe in the power you hold within yourself. Accept your role as co-creator of life. Recognize and utilize the support team we all have available through the spirit world. Let your light shine. There is nobody standing in your way but you alone.

I have been channelling messages from spirit for years. I keep a journal for this very purpose. There are so many times along the journey of my SOULworks where I have lost my confidence or stumbled along the path. It was during these hard times when I looked to the spirit world for help and guidance. Included below is a collection of some of my journal entries over the course of my SOULworks. Not only did this divine wisdom help me to move forward along my own path, I believe they will also be an important part of your own journey.

--------◄◊►--------

The world is in fact changing. We have spent lifetime after lifetime evolving as souls to bring us to this very point in history. The world has been successful in so many ways. As a society, we have come so far and learned so much. But there are still a lot of deceptions and envy in this world causing great hardships. It is ordinary people from ordinary backgrounds who will be the change champions. You came into this lifetime for this very purpose, and you must take this task seriously. The world is depending on you to help awaken lost souls and bring light into the darkness.

View the world as a pyramid. It all began at the top of the pyramid with one, unified energy source. Slowly you began to break apart and distance yourselves from this universal energy you call heaven. The further and further you moved away from Source, the less connected you became and the less you could feel the presence of the divine. It is time to reclaim your oneness and move back into the power within, to climb that pyramid and rightfully take your place beside God.

Much planning and preparation has been put into this time. Before you were born, plans were made on how you would contribute to this movement and help embrace the future. We cannot continue to do things the way society has become: jealous, no gratitude, lack of love, and no direction. You actually have to slow down and stop living in fast forward. Conserve your energies for what really matters. Love, healing energies, and oneness are not just catch phrases. It is the divine path to a truly blessed life.

Now is not the time to be bashful, modest or doubtful. You must reach out and change lives. Help heal the world. You will succeed and you have a very large angelic support team helping and cheering you on. Listen to your inner self and not your ego, that is always fearful and stressed. Connect your energy into one divine power, so your ability to manifest positive outcomes will become even stronger. If you can remove the fear, it will help shed light and healing energies. Do not think for one minute you are not affecting change.

⸻⋖◍⋗⸻

You have everything within you to take the next steps forward. Take a leap of faith. You will start to be able to do things you never thought possible. Your spiritual guides and the universal energy will support you.

⸻⋖◍⋗⸻

While society enters the dawn of the Golden Age of Enlightenment, I leave you with the lyrics of a song. My daughter wrote these thought-provoking words at the mere age of nine. Turns out she likes to connect with the spirit world for guidance too. After completion of the inspirational words, the lyrics were simply left on my bedside table for encouragement and confirmation of my own thoughts and beliefs. For the words echoed the feelings I had been having about my life's work and the need to actively step into my role as a healer and lightworker. Although my daughter remembers writing the first two lines, the rest of the message she bears no recollection of writing, even though the entire message was completed in her youthful handwriting. Channelled from the heavens above, these words of wisdom provide insights to the expansiveness of our world and the transition it has entered. Acknowledge the wisdom within.

> *I'm getting all crazy*
> *I gotta do what I gotta do*
> *Time is running by so fast*
> *Got no lives to last on what's coming by*
> *I gotta dance cause I've got the energy*
> *What's in my heart is what I believe*
> *A hundred worlds in a galaxy.*
> *Makenna Heistad, age 9*

Your Move:

❑ **Nourish your soul.** You literally thirst for more time spent on your life purpose, and the more time you can focus on your development, the better. It will improve your health, energy, and joy. This is the best investment you can make for your future. The universe has heard your prayers and the transition is already in progress. Your cravings for spirituality will increase until the shift becomes second nature. Use your own healing abilities to help the process. The more time you spend releasing negative energies, being in fresh air, and focusing on your goals, the quicker you will achieve them. Start using your healing abilities to help others release, cleanse, and awaken to their true essence. You are a breath of fresh air to this world. Recognize your soul potential. Step into your role.

❑ **Honor who you are.** Always honor who you are, where you came from, and what you have accomplished. You are a child of God and a carrier of the Light. You are not only qualified, but are very powerful and fully ready to activate your own SOULworks. Continue to think positively, open yourself up to the help and support of others, and remember that this is who you are meant to be. This is your destiny. As you take your leap of faith, the Universe will too. Everything will fall into place at an accelerated speed. Remember to watch for the signs and ideas that enter your thoughts. Spirit is communicating with you even more, now that you have acknowledged their presence and expanded the lines of communication. The spirit world has your back and your best interests in mind. They will support your own SOULworks.

❑ **Answer the call.** Listen to your inner wisdom and answer your divine call. You already are connected with spirit and have access to the universal energy. What you need to do is trust and practice your skills. Let the light within you shine with no inhibitions. The world needs to see the brightness that surrounds you. Your soul has always been strong, but to let it shine through your earthly body is a huge achievement. Congratulations on the official opening of your own SOULworks.

❑ **Blessed be.** Please ask God to bless and support your SOULworks. However, the true blessing is you and your willingness to expand your gifts. There will come a time when you will look back at your life's work and realize what a true blessing you have been to the world. Honor that.

Preface to the second book of the SOULworks series

Evolving your SOULworks: A Miraculous Journey
by Lauren Heistad

The following is a preview of Chapter One

Book 2, Chapter 1: The Sandman

Today we live in a society vastly intertwined and interconnected through the World Wide Web. The Internet has undeniably and remarkably altered the way we seek information, converse with loved ones, conduct research, share resources, send messages, and interact with strangers from across the globe. This communication tool has virtually accelerated our society into the Information Age, and this remarkable new era of technology has bridged a gap that was otherwise unavailable for data and knowledge dissemination. Or so we thought. [Enter the Sandman...]

I have an old friend. You know the type. The kind you used to see on a regular basis and yet, somehow over time you slowly drifted apart. This particular friend, who I will refer to as Trevor, had not been in my life for many years. We lived in separate communities, had our own separate families, separate interests, separate lives - you get the idea. There had literally not been any communication between the two of us for many, many years. At the time, we were not even linked via the usual online social media options, meaning we did not "connect" via posts, photo uploads or random updates on what was going on in each other's lives. We had simply become disconnected in all respects.

However, despite our distance in both miles and communication in general, I started to have weird dreams about this friend. Now, I have a lot of strange dreams while in the middle of a deep slumber, so for me to say this set of dreams was truly out there is pretty remarkable. However, these dreams were definitely out there.

In each dream, Trevor was trying to take his own life. In his basement, at his place of work - the locations changed slightly each time, but the actual dreams were always the same. On every occasion within the dreams, Trevor was in utter despair with a noose around his neck and crying out to the heavens for help. It was certainly a devastating sight to bear witness to. But it was also during those cries for help that I would jump into action. Just like some kind of freaky comic book hero, I would instantly respond to the distress signal and come to his rescue. I would pull Trevor off to the side, provide him comfort, adamantly declare I would not let him jump, and literally tell him it was not his time to go home to heaven, while uttering the words, "Not today my friend. Not today."

Each time I would hold my dear friend within that dream for as long as needed. Like taking part in some type of weird and surreal virtual world, I would watch the scene unfold and work to interrupt his suicide attempt until someone came into the room to provide assistance or enough time had passed for Trevor to change his mind for yet another day. Although every dream finished with a happy ending, every time I was presented with the vivid encounter, I would wake up and become a little more anxious about my dear old friend.

These dreams were very sporadic, but incredibly memorable and vivid just the same. Three times within a two-year span I dreamed of Trevor trying to commit suicide, and each time I provided the same service. I would speak to my friend at a soul level, take him off to the side away from the drama of the situation, and reassure him I was and always would be there for him.

Of course, in the morning, this was never really the case; I was never truly there for him. Come sunrise I would simply go about my own life, never reaching out to contact him, and truly never putting much thought into the meaning behind the dreams, beyond "well that was weird!" The first two dreams, that is. The third dream was definitely the charm. Following the third encounter of alarmingly watching Trevor struggle with life and consider another suicide attempt, I finally started to ponder the dreams. Perhaps he was literally calling out for help. Perhaps he was suffering and could really use a friend. Upon reflection of this concept, I received what I have learned to accept as my formal confirmation from spirit – a wave of energy flowed through me from head to toe and back again in a quick and fluent tidal wave. With nothing but a simple surge of energy that was totally tangible, spirit confirmed that this was in fact an outcry for help and that my services were certainly needed. Not a wonderful scenario to receive confirmation on, but confirmation nonetheless. So I followed the nudges from spirit, swallowed my pride, set aside my fears of being wrong, and I simply reached out to Trevor.

The first time I contacted Trevor was the day after I woke up from the third dream of the series. Being the strong communication type, Intuitive Healer, and a true spokesperson for spirit, I did what any brave and concerned soul of my generation would do: I sent him an e-mail. Yup, that is right. No phone call, no visit, just a quick electronic message. In the body of the text, I indicated I was not sure what was going on with him or his life, but that I felt I was supposed to help him. I indicated I was aware of three low points in his life where I felt depression was a problem for him, and urged him to contact me so we could further discuss and work it out. I then simply hit the send button and awaited a reply. And waited. And waited.

Perhaps I had insulted him, I thought to myself. Perhaps he felt great and was laughing at my absurd observation and forwardness. Perhaps I overstepped my boundaries. Perhaps the dreams were meaningless. Perhaps, perhaps, perhaps...

It was at this point I called my guides and angels for help. I acknowledged my deepest fears, reiterated my willingness to help out if there was anything I could do, and then stubbornly (once again out of fear of being wrong) suggested that if it was important for me to help Trevor and that if he was not going to respond to my message, then the Powers that Be should find another way for us to connect.

[Enter a divine connection.] A day after spewing all my thoughts and demands out to my guides, I was contacted by Trevor's wife. Although I had seldom talked to this lady, or connected with her in any way, she sent me a distinct request for help. In her e-mail, she expressed concerns for her husband, admitted to not knowing if or how I could help, and then humbly asked I provide some type of assistance. I responded right away, bringing awareness to the message I had sent a week earlier. This time, instead of just sending e-mails back and forth, I offered to drive down to meet with Trevor, suggesting that I had time to get together the following week.

Upon reflection of the e-mails and my offer of help, Trevor was brought into the loop and was grateful for the outreach (apparently, he was not checking the original account I had used). When asked if I could provide help the following week, Trevor responded in an honest and truthful fashion that I will never forget: "Yes, please come and help, but can you come tomorrow? I don't think I will be here by next week." His response brought clarity and urgency to the situation. Although I had no idea how I was going to help, it was becoming more and more apparent that I would.

When I arrived the next morning, I was greeted by a nervous and hesitant old friend whose demeanor changed the minute I walked in the door. He joked that I had come all that way to see how crazy he had become, and I reciprocated by teasing I had in fact come all that way to show him how crazy I always was. Years of being apart and the awkwardness of the situation just melted away as we reconnected at a soul level and we both instantly felt at ease.

Now I do not want to oversimplify the process of spiritual healing, but it literally took only thirty minutes of channelling loving energy from the spirit world to undo over ten years of depression for Trevor. What had been attempted through many other means including therapy, counseling, and medication had been shifted in a holy instant with the divine. And that is exactly why I continue to follow my inner guidance, work with spirit, speak my truth, and channel healing energies from the heavens.

I allow my body and energy field to be utilized by the spiritual realm and help direct the energy where needed. I create a portal with my intentions through which the energy can flow. Even though our earthly minds may not be able to fully understand the process or interconnectivity occurring, spirit is most certainly present to inspire our lives for the better. The energy does go exactly where it is needed and helps to bring changes on levels we cannot even begin to fully comprehend. But we can literally *feel* the change. We can feel the shifts that occur when spirit is brought into the equation and given the opportunity to evolve our life experience here on Earth. In fact, from that day forward, Trevor started to feel better. His depression lifted, his mood changed, and he literally got his life back.

My dear friend had suffered depression for years and was having trouble moving forward with his life. As it turns out, Trevor had three distinct low points at the times and locations I had dreamed about. He had truly and sincerely needed my help. In fact, my visions were not dreams at all; they were glimpses of his reality.

However, what I had yet to understand and fully grasp until our visit, was that I had already been providing help. You see, while talking with Trevor about his depression, he confided (although adding a disclaimer that he was not sure I would believe him), that three times in the past two years he had attempted to hang himself. Each of those three times, it was as if an invisible force entered the room, pulled him off to the side, provided comfort, and said, "Not today my friend. Not today."

Evolving your SOULworks

I love the Internet, social media, and the advancements of technology. I love the way our society has created the ability to access information at our fingertips and can virtually connect with anyone, anywhere, anytime. However, a quick reality check begs us to realize we have always had this ability. We have always been connected. We have always had access to the infinite wisdom and knowledge of the divine. It is not some newfangled techno gadget that is powering this interconnectivity. This connection is not reliant on an electrical power supply or a hard drive. It is powered by the divine and reliant on our ability to open our hearts and minds to spirit. We can literally connect with any soul, both of this world and of the spirit realms. The connection is instantaneous and infinite.

In my experience with Trevor, he never sent one e-mail, placed one phone call or made any attempt whatsoever to connect with me in physical form. However, I heard his call for help and responded just the same. Far be it from me to try to explain or fully understand the scope of what occurred those three nights, but also far be it from me to try to deny or dismiss that they happened. I heard Trevor call for help in the middle of the night, from miles away, while submerged deep within a dream state with the Sandman. Furthermore, within that lucid dream, I responded to his needs and held him in my arms until help could arrive.

Let us not overlook the sheer magnitude of this event or its possible implications. Ask and you shall receive. Look and you shall find. When a child of God called out to the heavens at his greatest time of need, I, a mere person and fellow child of God, was sent there to respond. I was the one who received his distress call and created a positive change in a loved one's life. I was the angel in the night that helped calm the storms. I was the invisible force that made a difference. I was, and I am, part of the divine. And so are you. As it is in Heaven, so it is on Earth.

We are all powerful, divine souls capable of so much more than we could ever begin to fathom. We are all connected and have the power within us to create change, to connect with loved ones from a distance, and to bring healing to our world. And heal it we will. Thanks be to God.

Your Move:

Here is where the journey of this book ends and life continues my dear friend. Not because I am trying to hide the information from you or have you buy my next book (although I would love it if you would). At this point, I simply do not understand how to comprehend or teach what I have learned in regards to this story. And so the journey continues, the learning expands, and our minds and souls evolve together.

Please understand no one comes into this game of life with all the answers. We must first engage in the game to learn how to make our next move. We must state our intentions, trust in the process and know that when our souls are ready, the stars will align and the next chapter of the adventure will unfold. I myself, cannot wait.

To you my dear ones, I send energy, encouragement, and loving intentions until we meet again and continue this journey. The time is near.

ABOUT THE AUTHOR

Lauren Heistad is an adept teacher of the spiritual arts, trance healer, psychic medium, and inspirational speaker.

In addition to a lifetime of unique spiritual encounters and healing experiences, Lauren has actively expanded her own awareness to understand, embrace, and teach how to fully utilize these profound moments of interconnectivity for the betterment and evolution of humanity. Utilizing her own naturally developed techniques and understandings, Lauren provides individual and group healing services, teaches others about energy healing, and proactively inspires others to understand and believe in their God-given abilities to make a positive impact in our world. After more than 25 years of personal experiences, Lauren officially launched her spiritual practice on September 11, 2011, and in 2013 opened her first SOULworks Sacred Healing Centre in Saskatoon, Saskatchewan, Canada. This modern day spiritual facility provides a tranquil space for people to experience and expand their own connection with spirit.

For more information on Lauren and her work, visit www.laurenheistad.com and www.soulworks.pro

CPSIA information can be obtained
at www.ICGtesting.com
Printed in the USA
LVOW10s0446110717

540884LV00009B/17/P